Report of the Confidential Inquiry into Homicides and Suicides by Mentally Ill People

Steering Committee of the Confidential Inquiry into Homicides and Suicides by Mentally Ill People

1996

© 1996 Royal College of Psychiatrists, 17 Belgrave Square, London SW1X 8PG

ISBN 0 902241 92 3

Published by the Royal College of Psychiatrists on behalf of the Steering Committee of the Confidential Inquiry into Homicides and Suicides by Mentally Ill People, Unit Office, PO Box 1515, London SW1X 8PL

Printed by Bell & Bain Ltd., Thornliebank, Glasgow

Contents

Acknowledgements

We would like to express thanks to the people who have helped us to identify cases, to the many others who have patiently filled in the questionnaires, to a wider group who have shown positive interest in the Inquiry and to the Department of Health and the Royal College of Psychiatrists who have supported the project. Thanks are due to Mr Charles Sharpe, Manager of the Biometrics Unit, The Institute of Psychiatry, for his invaluable advice and to Dr Emma Seymour for providing her editorial skills. Publication has depended on the expertise of the publishing department of the Royal College of Psychiatrists.

Inquiry personnel

Director
Dr William Boyd — Formerly Vice-Chairman, Mental Welfare Commission for Scotland, Physician Superintendent and Consultant Psychiatrist, Royal Edinburgh Hospital.

Administrator
Mrs Lynn Lacy — BA Hons Law

Steering Committee
Chairman
Professor Andrew Sims — Professor of Psychiatry, University of Leeds, President of the Royal College of Psychiatrists 1990–1993

Mr Andrew Brooker — Assistant Director, Hampshire Social Services; member of ADSS Mental Health Sub-Committee

Dr Rosemarie Cope — Consultant Forensic Psychiatrist, and Director, Reaside Clinic, Birmingham

Mr Stuart Fletcher — Former Regional General Manager, W.Midlands Health Authority taking lead on mental health issues

Ms Helen Hally — Executive Nurse Director, Lewisham & Guys Mental Health Trust

Professor Gethin Morgan — Professor of Mental Health, University of Bristol; author of Clinical Audit of Suicide & Other Unexpected Deaths, NHS Management Executive

Ms Marcia Rice — Health & Race Strategy Manager, West Lambeth Health Authority

Mrs Shirley Turner — Legal Member, Mental Health Act Commission 1983–1989; legal Member of Mental Health Review Tribunal (until mid-1994)

Representing the Department of Health
Miss Mary Hancock — Social Services Inspectorate
Dr David Kingdon — Health Care (Medical) Division (until mid-1994)
Mrs Elizabeth Parker — Mental Health & Community Care Division
Dr John Reed — Mental Health & Community Care Division

Foreword

Of all the possible outcomes following psychiatric illness and treatment, death is undoubtedly the worst; either the death of the patient or someone else at the patient's hand. Not surprisingly, therefore, it is mental health professionals themselves who are most keen to acquire any information which sheds light on these disasters. When Mr Stephen Dorrell, then Parliamentary Secretary for Health, proposed a national investigation into homicides by mentally ill people, I took the opportunity of requesting that the suicides of those who had received psychiatric treatment should also be included, hence this Inquiry considering both.

The Confidential Inquiry should not be thought of as an epidemiological study for obtaining purely statistical information as there are other, more effective, methods for data collection. However, the Inquiry, in seeking the opinions of all mental health professionals about those of their patients who subsequently kill themselves or another person, allows themes to be explored concerning the circumstances and antecedents of the death, reasons why it happened and ideas concerning future prevention. There are two substantial advantages in carrying out this survey on a national basis: by collecting national data the numbers are large enough to show trends for relatively rare events; it has not infrequently occurred that clinicians locally are more prepared to give information and opinions to the Inquiry, which is totally confidential and remote from their everyday practice, rather than have discussion amongst their own colleagues and managers.

The particular value of the Confidential Inquiry is therefore in demonstrating common patterns that have recurred in different parts of the country. One theme that has occurred both in this report and in our previous preliminary report on homicides by mentally ill people is that for many of the deaths there is a common factor of the patient's lack of compliance with treatment and with the services provided by mental health professionals. This is of course a wider issue than just the working practices of those involved in care; it involves what society at large is prepared to tolerate and wishes to impose on those who suffer from mental illness. No guidance to practitioners, however constraining, can have very much effect upon those who absolutely refuse to cooperate with their treatment. We have also observed a discrepancy between what informants say are their needs for being able to look after mentally ill people better and what the Inquiry has found on collecting national data. Very often individual practitioners have not stated their need for more resources and have not put this as a cause for the unfortunate death but the Inquiry has shown that staffing was inadequate or accommodation unsatisfactory. It is possible that practitioners do not ask for what they construe as being impossible. It is imperative that all trained staff are involved in continuing professional development to maintain their skills and learn new ways of working; however, it must be realised that some isolated practitioners will only then become aware of how inadequate their resources are for carrying out good quality care.

The tentative nature of this report emphasises the need for the Confidential Inquiry to continue its work, preferably over many years. The value of the data collected is cumulative and as the Inquiry becomes better known so it should be possible to collect a higher proportion of cases nationally. Once the basic data has been collected and described by the Inquiry it will become possible to concentrate on different aspects of homicide and suicide in subsequent reports by using the personal contacts and acquired methodology of the Inquiry. It is seen as an important part of the relationship with our informants, who come from all the mental health professional disciplines, that the Confidential Inquiry retains its independence both from the Department of Health and the Royal College of Psychiatrists although we fully acknowledge our gratitude to both these organisations and in practical terms we would not have been able to carry out our work without them. The Confidential Inquiry has the opportunity to confirm or refute findings from many local studies and then to take particular aspects of antecedence to homicide or suicide risk management, and consider them in more detail.

The work of the Inquiry will have been valueless unless it is translated into action. For ease of carrying out our recommendations we have added a summarising section entitled Action which lists possible strategies directed at the Department of Health, commissioning authorities, Trust management, and clinicians. Our conclusions are not necessarily proven to the extent of being irrefutable but as they broadly reflect accumulated wisdom from other studies and reports drawing on different methodologies we offer them as a contribution to this important area of debate.

Andrew Sims
Chairman
December 1995

Summary

The Confidential Inquiry into Homicides and Suicides by Mentally Ill People was set up in 1992 by the Department of Health following consultation with the Royal College of Psychiatrists.

The remit of the Inquiry is:

- to enquire into the circumstances leading up to and surrounding homicides and suicides committed by people under the care of, or recently discharged by, the specialist psychiatric services
- to identify factors in the patient's management which may be related to the deaths
- to recommend measures designed to reduce the number of homicides and suicides by mentally ill people.

Methods of identifying the 39 cases of homicide identified from our search of Home Office files during the periods July 1992–December 1993 and September 1994–March 1995 and the 240 cases of suicide (between June 1993 and December 1994) scrutinised by the Inquiry are outlined in Section III, Method of Inquiry. The principles of confidentiality and anonymity along which the Inquiry proceeded are described. Data were gathered through the use of questionnaires which were supplemented by respondents' individual comments and observations. The detailed description of the findings is in Section IV.

Section V, Discussion, does not purport to offer a blueprint for managing mentally ill people at risk of committing homicide of suicide but does outline some wider themes which allow generalisation from individual cases. Despite the similarities between incidents, each death is at the end of a complex trajectory of unique circumstances.

Although there appears to be scope for altering aspects of clinical practice, the Inquiry found little evidence of any mismanagement or neglect precipitating deaths. The Inquiry did identify some key problems, however. These include:

- failures of communication between professionals
- lack of clarity about care plans
- lack of time for face-to-face contact with patients
- the need for additional staff training
- poor compliance with treatment by the sample group
- insufficient use of legal powers to supervise at risk patients.

Section VI offers conclusions and recommendations. Key recommendations include:

- strengthening risk assessment skills in clinical teams
- increasing face-to-face contact time with patients
- supporting the development of genuine multi-disciplinary teams

- developing better systems for communication between professionals and between professionals and families
- raising awareness about appropriate uses of legal powers under the Mental Health Act 1983 through further training
- ensuring that treatment environments are acceptable to patients.

Meeting these recommendations will mean that commissioning authorities will have to consider reallocating more resources to the care of severely mentally ill people.

Appendix 1, An overview of homicide and suicide by mentally ill people, places such homicides and suicides in context. Appendices 2–5 list selected publications and examples from the questionnaires and correspondence.

I. Action

The recommendations of section VI are listed according to their topic. In this section they are briefly summarised according to who would be required to implement the recommendations.

Department of Health

1   The relationship between the consultant psychiatrist and the key worker caring for patients resident outside hospital should be clarified.
2   The Department of Health should ensure that there is regular monitoring of the availability of trained staff, of an appropriate range of accommodation within and outside hospital, and of continuing education for all grades and professions of mental health staff.
3   If the Mental Health (Patients in the Community) Act is to have maximum benefit, careful guidance and training of staff will be required. The impact of the Act will need careful monitoring.
4   The Confidential Inquiry has a continuing role in collecting information and surveying opinions of clinicians.

Commissioning Authority

1   Additional resources are required for the care of the severely mentally ill; this is especially necessary to supervise non-compliant patients in the community.
2   An adequate number of consultant psychiatrists, trained mental health nurses and occupational therapists should be provided for the needs of people with severe mental illness both in hospital and outside. Clinical psychology should be available in multidisciplinary teams for the severely mentally ill.
3   There should be protocols covering exchange of information between mental health professionals and other agencies: general practitioners, social services, voluntary organisations and the criminal justice system.
4   Adequate number and diversity of in-patient beds and other accommodation must be available for the severely mentally ill.

Provider Trusts

1   The functioning of multidisciplinary teams must be facilitated by providing adequate staffing and clarifying the accountability of the consultant and the roles of other members.
2   Closer integration with Social Services is required in the provision of services.
3   Information exchange protocols with other agencies should be incorporated

within operational policies, including social services and general practice.

4   Each Trust should ensure that locally agreed policies concerning CPA, Supervision Register and supervised discharge are available and adhered to with a view to improving continuity of care.

5   All staff coming into contact with severely mentally ill patients should be involved in continuing professional development, should receive training in risk assessment and management, and in ethical and clinical aspects of the Mental Health Act.

6   There should be provision for the appropriate involvement of families in the treatment of the severely mentally ill.

Mental Health Professional Organisations

1   All mental health professionals have a responsibility to maintain their knowledge and skills through continuing education, especially for risk assessment and management. Professional organisations should ensure that they institute training programmes and set standards and that their members avail themselves of these.

2   Similarly training should be provided on ethical and clinical aspects of the Mental Health Act.

3   Mental health professions should receive training in the provision of appropriate methods of treatment and support for the families of severely mentally ill people.

4   Treatment methods for those with personality disorders require evaluation. There should be teaching on validated methods of treatment.

Mental Health Clinicians

1   For every patient a care plan should be recorded in the case notes and regularly updated.

2   Mental health professionals should strive to reduce non-compliance by providing continuity of care and by adhering to Trust policies.

3   Local audit should measure the extent and quality of direct staff:patient contact.

4   Local audit should address levels of non-compliance.

5   Mental health professionals should strive to maintain the involvement of families in the care of severely mentally ill people.

6   Among mental health professionals some should be trained in family intervention.

7   The risk of disaster occurring at times of change in the patient's circumstances should be recognised and the care plan adapted appropriately.

II. Introduction

Remit of the Inquiry

The Confidential Inquiry into Homicides and Suicides by Mentally Ill People was set up by Mr Stephen Dorrell M.P., at that time Parliamentary Under Secretary of State for Health, following discussions with the Royal College of Psychiatrists. The Inquiry is funded by the Department of Health and began its work in January 1992. The conclusions and recommendations of the Inquiry are independent of both the Department of Health and the Royal College of Psychiatrists.

The remit of the Inquiry is:

- to enquire into the circumstances leading up to and surrounding homicides and suicides committed by people under the care of, or recently discharged by, the specialist psychiatric services
- to identify factors in the patient's management which may be related to the deaths
- to recommend measures designed to reduce the number of homicides and suicides by mentally ill people.

The Inquiry was set up in response to widespread concern about cases of homicide committed by psychiatric patients. Psychiatrists and other mental health professionals have also been concerned about suicides among patients under their care and it was agreed to include these deaths in the Inquiry.

The decision to study such deaths at a national level received considerable support given the debate among those providing mental health services about the adequacy of the treatment and supervision of patients, both in hospital and after discharge into the community.

The Inquiry scrutinised the management of individuals from the moment of first contact with the specialist psychiatric services until after their discharge by the consultant psychiatrist from specialist psychiatric care into the care of other agencies, including general practitioners.

The Inquiry's terms of reference specified that we should examine patients who were still under care, or who had been "recently discharged". We have taken "recently discharged" to mean that we should look at homicides and suicides by patients within one year of their discharge from specialist care. We have also decided that the term "specialist psychiatric service" should not include care provided by mental health professionals working independently of a consultant psychiatrist and the multi-disciplinary team.

The White Paper *The Health of the Nation*[1] was published shortly after the setting up of the Inquiry. The Health of the Nation set targets for:

- improving significantly the health and social functioning of mentally ill people
- reducing the overall suicide rate by at least 15% by the year 2000.
- reducing the suicide rate of severely mentally ill people by at least 33% by the year 2000.

The increased interest in suicide audit following the publication of *The Health of the Nation* has meant that providers of mental health care have been encouraged to set up review systems by purchasers and others. These developments, valuable in themselves, have nonetheless complicated the system of identification and information-gathering which we had already begun to develop, particularly in relation to sensitive information coming directly and confidentially from clinicians to the Director of the Inquiry. There is a risk that parallel inquiries, at local and at national levels, could prove to be a burden for clinicians.

From time to time we were invited by media representatives to make comments on highly publicised cases, such as that of Christopher Clunis[2] or the tragedy at London Zoo involving Ben Silcock. We decided, however, that the contribution which this Inquiry should attempt to bring to the debate on whether there was a connection between such incidents and the effectiveness of psychiatric services must be based on evidence from a broad survey of a large number of cases. It is for others to base their opinions and recommendations on the findings from individual cases.

Other Confidential Inquiries

The decision to set up the Confidential Inquiry into Homicides and Suicides by Mentally Ill People was influenced by the knowledge that other Confidential Inquiries were already established:

- The Confidential Inquiry into Peri-operative Deaths began as a survey of three regions, and was expanded in 1987 to cover the whole of the United Kingdom
- The Confidential Enquiry into Maternal Deaths published a first report covering the period 1985–87
- The Confidential Enquiry into Stillbirths and Deaths in Infancy and the Confidential Inquiry on Genetic Counselling have been set up more recently.

None of the Confidential Inquiries claim to be an epidemiological research project. This would require controls and population data which are not available. However, the Inquiries all seek to bring together data and experience from clinical practice in order to make recommendations which will influence and improve the service provided.

Reports of local inquiries into deaths by homicide or suicide

At the outset of the Inquiry there was already available a number of reports which

13

had followed inquiries into individual cases of homicide and suicide among mentally ill people. Some of these reports were published and widely distributed, while others were confidential reports commissioned by management. We received copies of the confidential reports in response to our request for information from Regional Medical Officers, whose assistance we gratefully acknowledge.

What is striking in reading these reports of local inquiries is the extent to which similar themes recur and similar recommendations are made. For our own use we listed items which seemed to indicate recurring areas of concern in the reports of local inquiries and we reproduce them in the Discussion below. A comprehensive review of the recommendations of 17 inquiries carried out between 1985–1994 is now available[3].

Effects of recent major changes in psychiatric practice

This Inquiry has been conducted against a backdrop of changes in psychiatric practice. New management systems underpin the provision of clinical care, resources are shifted from hospital to community, and new legislation alters the nature of clinical work. The introduction of the Patients' Charter, the higher profile of voluntary groups, and the introduction of advocacy for less competent patients, have all had their effects. The White Paper *Caring for People*, and the National Health Service and Community Care Act 1990, served to alert people to the new responsibilities of local social services. The role of housing departments in the overall care of the mentally ill and those with learning disabilities has also been emphasised[4].

The White Paper *The Health of the Nation*, in particular, has focused attention on prevention of suicide. This has resulted in a great variety of local responses with effects on suicide rates which cannot easily be assessed because of the small numbers involved. In addition, the high profile given in Parliament, in the media and in psychiatric literature to community care for psychiatric patients may have influenced clinical practice over the period of time during which the Inquiry has been collecting data. In brief, the Confidential Inquiry has based its conclusions on data which have been changing in response to altered circumstances even during the Inquiry's working life.

About this report

The report should be of particular interest to:
- mental health professionals
- purchasers of mental health services
- providers of mental health services
- voluntary mental health organisations
- policy-makers.

This report results from the Inquiry's review of cases of homicide and suicide by mentally ill people as specified in the Inquiry's terms of reference.

Appendix 1 provides an overview of homicide and suicide by mentally ill people. Other appendices list selected publications and give examples of the questionnaires

14

and of the correspondence. The main report offers an account of the **Method of inquiry** and **Findings** followed by a **Discussion** of the key findings and a section of **Conclusions and recommendations**.

Key points have been highlighted in bold print in the text.

The aims of the report, in accordance with the Inquiry's terms of reference, are:

- to give an account of the circumstances surrounding the homicides and suicides (Findings of the Inquiry)
- to offer views on factors in patients' management which may be related to the deaths (Discussion)
- to make recommendations designed to reduce the number of homicides and suicides by mentally ill people (Conclusions and recommendations).

A number of important caveats should be stressed at the outset:

- the sample is not representative and the Inquiry has no claims to be an epidemiological research project
- despite the similarities between incidents of homicide and suicide, each such death is at the end-point of a complex and unique trajectory
- although we have attempted to draw conclusions from our information we have not attempted to offer a blueprint for changing clinical practice
- although there appears to be scope for altering aspects of practice (such as staffing ratios) we have found little evidence of any mismanagement or neglect precipitating deaths
- we hope that this report will be of use in encouraging purchasers, providers and clinicians to develop local solutions to local problems.

III. Method of Inquiry

Identification of cases

Homicide

In the Confidential Inquiry's Preliminary Report on Homicide[5] the method of identifying cases which fell within the remit of the Inquiry was explained.

A process was established to identify all homicide cases notified to the Home Office S1 Division in which any previous psychiatric contacts were noted. With the assistance of the Home Office C3 Division we also listed all persons committing homicide who subsequently became the responsibility of the specialist services under the powers of the Mental Health Act 1983. This list covered all mentally disordered offenders subject to hospital orders with restriction on discharge under sections 37/41 of the Mental Health Act, as well as remanded and sentenced prisoners transferred to hospital under sections 48 and 47 respectively.

The Home Office files of all the cases thus identified were examined to ascertain whether or not they fell within the remit of the Inquiry. We carried out detailed examination of every case-file referred to us. Sometimes it was immediately apparent that the case fell within our remit, for example when the homicide was carried out by an individual while an in-patient in a psychiatric hospital or shortly after discharge to out-patient care. It was less easy to ascertain the psychiatric status of someone whose only contact had been as an out-patient and whose supervision had been less intensive, but every effort was made to include such cases also.

The essential information to be gleaned from the files, apart from the personal details, was the name of the consultant looking after the patient before the event. Sometimes this name was not immediately available but could be obtained by approaching the consultant psychiatrist currently responsible for the individual's care.

When contact had been established with the relevant clinical team we made use of a questionnaire, similar to that used in the suicide inquiry, but modified to obtain information about the circumstances of the homicide and the relationship with the victim. This was sent initially to the consultant psychiatrist. However, once we had gained experience in using the questionnaire we began to make contact not only with the consultant but also with other professional staff who had been involved in treating the patient.

We emphasise here that the objective of the Inquiry is to identify individuals whose psychiatric care prior to the offence of homicide can be examined in detail. Only a small proportion of cases where mental disorder was evident at trial came within the remit of the Inquiry and these cases in turn formed only a small proportion of all homicides. In spite of the understandable concern about murders committed by people in the care of the psychiatric services, whether in hospital or in the community, it is important to maintain some sense of proportion between the numbers involved and the total number of homicides.

Our task was to review the psychiatric care which had been provided for our sample and, in the words of our terms of reference, "to identify factors in the patient's management which may be related to the deaths".

This report is based on the 39 cases of homicide (identified from our search of Home Office files during the periods July 1992–January 1994 and September 1994–March 1995) in England which fell within the remit of the Inquiry.

Suicide

We looked carefully at methods for collecting cases and received valuable advice from individual Coroners and their staff. We concluded that it would be impossible to ensure that a complete national series could be guaranteed from these sources. Although we did not see it as our task to obtain comprehensive data at national level on precise numbers of suicide episodes, we did require to be confident that our cases came from all geographical areas and were thus representative of the country as a whole.

Use of mechanisms to collect data at district or regional levels was thwarted by the changing administrative structure of the NHS. However, a system calling upon the assistance of consultant psychiatrists who had already identified themselves to the Research Unit of the Royal College of Psychiatrists as audit representatives in their own districts has proved successful and has brought us cases from every region in England.

We asked our contacts to give us the name of any patient who had recently died by suicide whilst under the care of, or recently discharged from, the specialist psychiatric services. We also requested the name of the consultant who had been involved in the patient's care immediately prior to death. We then made direct contact with this named consultant.

Recognising the variations in audit practice around the country, we encouraged our audit representatives to use all possible means of identifying cases. These could include contact with Coroners' offices, with local pathologists and with Directors of Public Health. Having established a reporting mechanism in the spring of 1993, data collection began formally in June of that year. **The present report is based on the 240 cases where data collection was completed by December 1994.**

We have now received notification of in excess of 950 individuals who were thought to have killed themselves up to the end of October 1995. A small proportion of these were excluded from our study because they did not come within our remit. The majority of these 950 cases, however, result from the rapid increase in the cases now being made known to us. Thus, since January 1995 we have been notified of 714 cases in 10 months. We continue to identify new cases and to make contact with the clinicians involved in the care of these people prior to death.

In the course of the Inquiry we have been asked whether we could include cases of attempted suicide in our survey but this would clearly involve a massive increase in case-finding. We have also been asked to consider the inclusion of sudden unexpected deaths occurring among people being treated within the psychiatric service. This would be much more feasible as it would involve the same method of case-identification as has been established in the study of suicide.

Confidentiality

An important feature of the Inquiry is the opportunity for those most closely involved in the treatment of the patient to give details of the case in complete confidence, and to indicate whether they believe that any different way of caring for the patient might have reduced the likelihood of the suicide. This guaranteed confidentiality is similar to that offered by the Confidential Enquiries into Peri-operative Mortality and Maternal Death.

Such confidential details and opinions had often not been voiced at the local review of the death, and might not even have appeared to be of major importance at that time. When examined in the context of national responses, however, these details and opinions may offer valuable information.

The confidentiality of the Inquiry was emphasised in all our contacts with individual practitioners in response to three areas of concern:

- the insistence that there should be no possibility that individual patients might be identified in any report arising from the Inquiry
- the need for reassurance that potential criticisms of the case-management, of other members of the clinical team or of the local psychiatric service should remain a private matter between the respondent and ourselves
- the concern that the information given to us should be safeguarded from any later legal proceedings where our files might be open to scrutiny.

It was explained to all those expressing concern about confidentiality that our aim was to seek out general themes rather than to investigate individual cases. Our office procedures therefore involved the removal of personal identification of cases once we had obtained all necessary information for the Inquiry. In practice this has meant that we retained the papers showing names of patient, consultant psychiatrist and other staff involved in the case only until we had obtained all necessary responses. At this point, all such identifying data were removed.

Regardless of any future co-ordination which may develop between local and national auditing in an effort to reduce the demands on clinicians, it is essential that this opportunity for confidential reporting should remain.

Questionnaires

Our questionnaires were developed from one used in the Bristol in-patients survey[6]. We adapted the questionnaires to make them appropriate for both homicides and suicides occurring among in-patients, out-patients and recently discharged patients. Examples from the six questionnaires are provided in Appendix 3. It is intended that the questionnaires should be modified in the light of the responses received, and to take account of changing priorities among the topics already covered. We are keen that these questionnaires should be available for local use, for this would reduce pressure on clinicians and avoid duplication of effort.

However there will be occasions when practitioners are more prepared to divulge important information to a Confidential Inquiry which rapidly destroys its individual records and identification than to local management.

Review of individual comments and observations

The collection of structured questionnaire responses was only one part of our survey. **We attached equal importance to the personal comments which we received from the clinicians whom we had contacted.** We wanted to discover whether a better outcome might have been achieved through:

- different approaches to the clinical management of the patient
- different procedures within the multi-disciplinary team
- different psychiatric service provision
- different community facilities.

We therefore invited our respondents to make additional observations relating to any of the sections of the questionnaire. Giving respondents a further opportunity to look critically at all the circumstances surrounding the death of their patient, we asked

> Apart from any recommendations described above, please tell me whether with hindsight you consider that there are any other ways in which the likelihood of this death might have been reduced.

We wished to establish whether these individual and subjective responses, when considered together, might indicate that there were recurring themes and patterns which required to be highlighted in the report of our Inquiry.

It is striking that in many cases our respondents, even with the benefit of complete confidentiality and with the opportunity to distance themselves from the distressing outcome which they were reporting, felt that the death could not have been prevented by any measure which might have been adopted by the clinical team or the psychiatric service.

There was a danger that the multitude of additional comments written in alongside the questionnaires might be extracted and then considered out of context. If repeated in more than one area of the questionnaire or by more than one member of the clinical team certain observations might receive undue weight. We tried to avoid such a possibility by ensuring that every questionnaire was examined by the same individual (Dr Boyd). Dr Boyd extracted all written comments, thereafter allocating them under one of six headings:

1. Clinical management & staff responsibilities

2. Code of practice and guidelines
3. Family involvement
4. Important life events for patient before death
5. Recommendations following review
6. Compliance with treatment.

Respondents to the questionnaires

While our first contact was with the consultant psychiatrist responsible for the patient's care immediately before the death, we were keen to obtain views from members of all mental health professions involved in the care of the patient prior to the death. Questionnaires identical to those sent to the consultant psychiatrist were therefore sent out to the other mental health staff known to have been involved in the case.

Contact with families of patients who kill themselves

In the initial stages of setting up this Inquiry, we considered how far it would be feasible to ask for the views of the families of patients in our study. Families were likely to have had close contact with the patient in the weeks before the death and would have formed their own opinion about the clinical management of the case and the treatment which had been provided. Their expertise in the minutiae of treatment methods might be limited, and their views might be distorted by the intensity of their grief. Nevertheless families ought to have the opportunity, like the professional carers, of helping us to understand whether any measures might have been taken to reduce the likelihood of the death.

It was difficult to develop a mechanism for contacting relatives. Members of the clinical team found it an uncomfortable experience to go over ground which had already been explored in the immediate aftermath of the death. They were reluctant to expose families to questions from the Inquiry which might open up recently healed wounds.

While we respected this viewpoint, we were soon made aware that there were people desperate to speak to someone about the circumstances of the death. We had to make it clear to them that our job was not to investigate individual cases, but it was very helpful to gain an overall impression of what families had felt about their experiences.

After we had spoken to a number of relatives about our dilemma we decided to approach potential contacts indirectly. We were given space in the spring 1995 edition of the journal for bereaved families, *The Compassionate Friends Newsletter*, to explain the work of the Inquiry (see Appendix 4).

The number of replies has been small, and not all those who telephoned us to express their feelings have been able to write about their experiences. **However, responses from families have raised important issues in a forceful way**.

Extension of the Inquiry to Scotland, Northern Ireland and Wales

In the Introduction it was explained that the Inquiry was set up by the Department of Health after discussion with the Royal College of Psychiatrists. However, we were encouraged to extend the Inquiry to Scotland, Northern Ireland and Wales once the initial survey in England was under way.

We have not, as yet, developed a system for identification of cases in Wales, but we are satisfied that support will be forthcoming from the Welsh Office and from clinical teams in the Principality.

Comparisons between the inquiries in England and those in Scotland, Northern Ireland and Wales where the legal framework, and the structure of medical and social services are somewhat different, may demonstrate interesting variations in the patterns of homicide and suicide, but this will only emerge in time.

IV. Findings of the Inquiry

We emphasise that the sample from which we obtain our data is not a comprehensive one. We do not claim that our cases are representative of all mentally ill people who have died by suicide or who have killed another person at a time when they were receiving psychiatric treatment or within a year of discharge from such treatment. Only when there is an effective national system for collecting such cases will it be proper to make sophisticated calculations based on the reported characteristics of individual patients. This should not prevent us, however, from setting down the details of the cases which have been brought to our notice as a first step towards a wider and more accurate review. We confirm that, in our survey of suicides, cases have been brought to us from every area of the country and from urban and rural communities.

The findings fall into four sections:

I   Homicides – England
II   Suicides – England
III Suicides – Scotland
IV   Suicides – Northern Ireland.

Each section is arranged in the following manner:

A   Demographic description
B   Psychiatric and social background
C   Circumstances immediately preceding the homicide/suicide
D   The homicide/suicide event
E   Review following the homicide/suicide
F   Review of personal comments and observations.

I   Homicides – England

In this report we make use of the 22 cases reviewed in our Preliminary Report on Homicide, examining in more detail the data obtained and adding to them a further 17 cases identified through our continued access to Home Office files. In the following paragraphs we give details of these **39** cases.

Thirty-six of these patients were in touch with the community psychiatric services at the time of the homicide, two were in-patients in psychiatric units, and one had been discharged from psychiatric care within 12 months of the death.

Questionnaires were sent out first to the consultant psychiatrist responsible for the patient immediately prior to the offence. Where the returned completed questionnaire gave the names of other staff involved with the patient, questionnaires were sent to these individuals.

In sending out the questionnaires we emphasised that we preferred to have the questionnaire returned incomplete rather then held back merely because of the absence of information on any one specific area of enquiry, and in drawing conclusions from returned questionnaires we have treated uncompleted items as "don't knows" rather than as negative responses.

Demographic description

Sex

Table 1 shows that males accounted for more than two thirds of our cases.

Age distribution

In age, individuals ranged widely from 17–62 (Table 2). There were more older subjects than are found among those guilty of homicide who are not mentally ill.

Marital status

Almost half of the group were single (see Table 3).

Employment

25 patients were unemployed, seven of these being unemployed through chronic ill health.

Ethnic group

Eighty per cent of patients, where ethnicity was mentioned, were Caucasian, 10% were Black Caribbean, and 5% were Black African. The ethnic group was not stated in 5% of cases.

Accommodation

Of the two in-patients, one was detained in a regional secure unit and the other in a hospital for people with learning difficulties. Among the 36 out-patients, 55% were living at home with others, 22% were living at home alone. Of the remaining 23% two were in lodgings, three were in local authority or health service accommodation, one in alternative accommodation and two were in unspecified accommodation.

Psychiatric and social background

Diagnosis

We asked respondents to use ICD–10 in reporting diagnosis, but in practice this was not always done. ICD–9 was used by some, and on a considerable number of occasions a diagnosis by name was used. We therefore took the primary diagnosis provided for us and allocated each case into one of six groups, making use of any further information in the questionnaire to confirm our decision. The six groups were:

1. Schizophrenia, paranoid psychosis (ICD–10, F20–29)
2. Affective Illness, manic-depressive psychosis, depression (ICD–10, F30–F39)
3. Neurosis, anxiety state, obsessional state, depressive reaction (ICD–10, F40–F48)
4. Personality disorders, alcoholism, drug misuse (ICD–10, F60–F69)
5. Organic disorder (ICD–10, F00–F09)
6. Diagnosis not given, no psychiatric diagnosis (one case).

Overall 41% of the cases were suffering from schizophrenia. However there were significant differences between men and women in the relative frequency of diagnoses. Among the males 55% had schizophrenia, 19% affective disorder and 26% personality disorder. Among the women 8% had schizophrenia, 75% affective disorder and 17% personality disorder (see Table 4).

In five of the men diagnosed as suffering from schizophrenia or paranoid psychosis a second diagnosis relating to personality disorder or drug misuse was made.

Previous contact with specialist psychiatric care

Twenty-four of the 39 patients had been involved in previous psychiatric care, and 19 of these had been in-patients. Sixteen patients had received specialist social work support.

Earlier episodes of aggression or self-harm

Sixty-six per cent of individuals had been involved in earlier episodes of violent or aggressive behaviour and 26% had received criminal convictions involving violence. Deliberate self-harm was reported in 38% of patients. Violent behaviour in other family members was noted in 11 cases and suicidal behaviour in three.

Physical illness

Only one individual had been subject to serious physical illness.

Circumstances immediately preceding the homicide

Clinical notes

We were concerned to know whether the clinical team had access to previous psychiatric history, particularly evidence of violent behaviour. Those responsible for the psychiatric care of these patients had access to previous case notes in 23 (58%) patients, and only in three cases was it indicated that case notes were not available.

Awaiting admission

There were no reports that any of these patients were awaiting a place as an in-patient, but in one case an appropriate place was not available and less suitable alternative arrangements had been made.

Detention under the Mental Health Act 1983

Six patients had been subject to sections of the Mental Health Act, but none was detained at the time of the homicide. Two patients had been detained under the Mental Health Act in the last one to three months and one patient during the previous three to six months. Of the five patients detained at some point during this episode of illness, one in-patient had been detained under section 37/41, two out-patients had been detained under section 3 and one under section 2. A fourth out-patient had received after care under section 117.

Care Programme Approach

It was reported that a care plan was in place for 16% of the out-patients, and in 48% cases it was reported that no plan had been implemented. However, the nomination of a key worker was made in 10 instances, six being nurses, three social workers, and one a doctor.

Stage of assessment

In 51% of the patients, treatment and care was said to be well established. Assessment of dangerousness had always been carried out by a psychiatrist member of the clinical team. Surprisingly, the presence of paranoid delusions as evidence of the seriousness of aggressive intent was recorded only in three cases, all of these being men suffering from schizophrenic illnesses.

Episodes of physical or verbal aggression

In 46% of cases it was indicated that the patient had shown aggression in the period of care leading up to the homicide but in 41% of cases no aggression had been reported, even when the patient had been questioned directly about this. Thirty-eight per cent of the total sample had also acknowledged suicidal feelings.

During this same period there had been changes in the observed intensity of aggressive feelings with apparent improvement in 26% of patients, no change in 5% and deterioration in 2%. However, difficulties in assessment were particularly obvious among the 20% of cases showing fluctuation.

In 23% of cases the staff had felt reassured by the improvement in mental state, while in 15% of cases they had remained concerned about the patient's aggression.

Alcohol or substance abuse

The use of alcohol or other non-prescribed substances immediately preceding the homicide was reported in 18% of cases.

Actions taken in response to risk of aggression

The most common action had been to seek greater supervision or to recommend hospital admission. However, on seven occasions when further action was being considered, it proved difficult to take precautions, usually because the patient did not wish to accept greater supervision or to have treatment as an in-patient. **In six cases the possibility of detaining a patient under the Mental Health Act 1983 was considered but not pursued. Five of these cases were discussed with the Approved Social Worker and in two of these cases there was a difference in professional opinion.** In both these cases the patients were beginning to accept the need for treatment.

Asked whether the levels of psychiatric staff had been adequate for satisfactory supervision, 20 replies indicated that staffing was adequate. These replies covered in-patients and out-patients. Only one reply dealing with an out-patient indicated inadequate staffing. However personal comments would seem to give a contrary impression (page 29).

Significant life events and relationships

Details of significant events in the patient's environment are described later, under **Review of individual comments and observations** (pages 27–29). Such events were said to be present in 14 cases, with break up in relationships (6) and loss of self-esteem (7) being the most frequently reported.

Aspects of personality

While 17 patients were said to have a good relationship with staff members, there was little evidence of good contact with other patients. We gained an impression of solitary individuals who frequently declined appointments and did not take prescribed medication.

Cooperation with treatment plans

At least seven patients had failed to cooperate in treatment plans and in one case discharge back to the GP was being arranged after the individual had failed to attend three out-patient appointments.

Thus among the 36 out-patients there were problems with supervision in 13 patients (36%) and with the administration of medicines in 15 patients (41%). In six instances (16%) the problems of supervision and administration of medicines occurred in the same patient.

The homicide event

Method

The most frequent causes of death were stabbing (17) and asphyxiation (seven) (Tables 5a–c).

The victim

Members of family were most at risk; 64% of all the homicides were of family members. Particularly this was true of female patients where 82% of homicides were of family members. Among the 12 women in the sample, nine had killed their own children, ranging in age from ten days to 13 years, eight of these nine patients had been diagnosed as suffering from a depressive illness and one from a personality disorder (Tables 6a and 6b).

Homicide of a total stranger was very unusual; three cases in all. Two of these three homicides were by males with schizophrenia and one by a male with a personality disorder.

Review following the homicide

A review of patient care was reported in only 25 cases out of the 39 (64%), always involving doctors, with participation from nurses, including community psychiatric nurses (22), social workers (8) and other staff on occasions. In answer to the question about whether there had been any difference of opinion among staff about the patient's management, 28 replies indicated no difference. In one in-patient case, nursing staff felt that their opinions about the patient had not been taken into account.

Review of personal comments and observations

The personal comments of the respondents are reviewed under six headings: Clinical management and staff responsibilities; Protocols and guidelines; Family involvement; Important life events for patient before death; Recommendations following review; Compliance with treatment.

The following paragraphs are based on consideration of 110 separate comments.

Clinical management and staff responsibility (26 comments)

This heading covers any comments about the general care and supervision of the patient, including broader issues affecting the services available to people with mental illness or mental disorder.

Staff often felt that the homicide had been totally unpredictable and that there had been no indicators of possible violence – "no suggestion of violence"; "not thought to be a danger to others". Where aggression had been seen it had been towards self or household articles rather than towards others.

In a number of cases the potential for violence had been acknowledged but action had not been possible, either because it was thought to be inappropriate – "not detained further because she was calmer and her partner accepted responsibility" – or because an immediate reaction was not feasible – "lack of beds prevented transfer to a secure unit"; "seen after overdose, offence occurred while awaiting out-patient appointment".

Only once was there evidence of disagreement between staff over the correct placement of a patient. One other report emphasised the difficulty of dealing with "a ward with mixed sexes and much behaviour disturbance".

Protocols and guidelines (7 comments)

Only a few comments were made, ranging from a very general instruction – "adapt hospital policy regarding the management of violence" to the more specific instruction – "defuse the situation, separate the subjects, give time-out, remove to seclusion". Other comments stressed the importance of treating the violent patient in a unit with a generous staff–patient ratio, and the need to document aggressive acts. There were no comments on guidelines for dealing with aggressive behaviour among patients living in the community.

Family involvement (16 comments)

It was reported that relatives on occasion had helped patients to remove themselves from treatment – "mother had instigated discharge from a secure unit". Some relatives had been afraid of outbursts to a point where they could not encourage the patient to attend the out-patient clinic. However, other comments touched on the good contact between staff and relatives.

Important life events for patient before homicide (12 comments)

Seven of these comments referred to a breakdown between the patient and a family member or partner – "husband going overseas"; "break-up with girl-friend".

Other items referred to problems at work, unpleasant remarks, and serious illness in a relative. Less information was available than in the equivalent section on suicide where a vivid picture is provided of a wide range of events (see pages 42–43).

Recommendations from review (33 comments)

Recommendations ranged very widely over many aspects of patient care. Although dealing with only one or two cases, some of these recommendations may have general applications. Recommendations included:

- improved communication between hospital staff and community staff
- quicker response to non-compliance
- involvement of fewer professionals in home visiting of mothers with babies and young children
- more frequent review of dangerousness.

One homicide resulted in a massive increase in physical security where, in the view of the respondent, increase in staff numbers would have been more appropriate.

The comments gave a general impression of concern about these sometimes very difficult cases. Nurses felt that staff levels on wards were pitched at a level too low to allow any therapeutic interaction with patients. Psychiatrists worried that suitable placements were not available. Overall, there was a need for greater coordination between social services and psychiatric services to ensure effective supervision and adequate specialist review.

Compliance with treatment (35 comments)

The greatest number of comments dealt with perceived difficulties resulting from the personality and the behaviour of the patient. A number of patients were represented as loners – "very solitary and unable to relate to others". As a consequence of this view it was considered difficult to engage this group in treatment.

Sometimes patients refused to accept arrangements offered them – "great reluctance to engage in any planning for attendance at day-centre or for admission"; "was always out when Health Visitor called". Others did not come for appointments or did not take prescribed medication, while a small number used prescribed medication while also taking illicit drugs. One comment indicated that a patient had been "instructed to continue medication and to report to a new GP and to the housing department", all of which he did not do.

II Suicides – England

Demographic description

We base the findings of this report on **240** cases occurring between June 1993 and December 1994. Many of these patients had been examined by only one clinician, usually the consultant psychiatrist, but others had been supervised by several members of the clinical team. We have attempted to obtain questionnaire responses from more than one source where this has seemed appropriate. We have examined a total of 416 questionnaires relating to the 240 cases identified. The number of questionnaires received for one patient ranges from one to seven, more than two questionnaires being returned more frequently for in-patients (Table 7).

The 240 cases divide into **154 (64%) out-patients, 53 (22%) in-patients and 33 (14%) patients discharged from specialist care during the year before death.**

As with homicides we emphasised in sending out the questionnaires that we preferred to have the questionnaire returned incomplete rather then held back merely because of the absence of information on any one specific area of enquiry, and in drawing conclusions from returned questionnaires we have treated uncompleted items as "don't knows" rather than as negative responses.

Sex

Males accounted for 64% of our cases (Table 8) and there were significantly more single male in-patients than females.

Age distribution

Our patients spanned the age groups from under 20 to over 70 (Table 9). The majority of males were aged less than 50 years. Of the 134 males who were out-patients or in-patients, 16 (12%) were under 25 years of age; 10 (14%) of the 70 females in these categories were under 25.

Marital status

Almost 50% of the patients were not married and 35% were married or co-habiting. When individuals in a relationship (married or cohabiting) were compared with those who were alone (single, separated, divorced or widowed) there were significantly more people living out of a relationship. Sixty-six per cent of individuals where marital details were given were classed as being alone.

Employment

The categories of employment were classified as "occupied" (full-time education, employed or self-employed), "unoccupied" (unemployed or unemployed through ill health) and "at home" (retired or housewife/husband). Of the 221 individuals about whom information was given, 61 (28%) were occupied, 105 (47%) were unoccupied and 55 (25%) were at home. Significantly more suicides fell into the unoccupied classification than the others. Sixty-three per cent of patients in the "unoccupied" group were unemployed, and the rest were unable to work due to chronic ill health.

Ethnic group

Ninety-one per cent of the patients where ethnicity was stated were Caucasian, 3% were Black Caribbean, 2% Black African and a further 2% of Indian or Pakistani origin. The ethnic group was not stated in 2% of cases (Table 10).

Accommodation

Among the 154 patients living in the community 74 (48%) were accommodated in their own home with others, 43 (28%) at home on their own, and 16 (10%) in lodgings or hostel. No information was available about 21 (14%) out-patients.

Of the 53 in-patients 77% were in wards designated as acute. Such wards were not normally locked, but about a quarter of them would be locked from time to time. **Often the wards were full or even, in 4 cases, overfull. In 19 (35%) cases wards had 25 or more beds, and wards with 36, 38 and 40 beds were reported.**

We asked about the staffing levels in the in-patient units. In three cases the nursing level was said to be unsatisfactory and on six occasions it was felt that the ratio between trained and untrained staff was inappropriate. There was, however, considerable variation between the ratios reported to us.

Psychiatric and social background

Diagnosis

We asked respondents to use ICD–10 in reporting diagnosis, but in practice this was not always done. ICD–9 was used by some, and a diagnosis by name was often used. We therefore took the primary diagnosis provided for us and allocated each case into one of six groups, making use of any further information in the questionnaire to confirm our decision. The six groups were:
1. Schizophrenia, paranoid psychosis (ICD–10, F20–29)
2. Affective illness, manic-depressive psychosis, depression (ICD–10, F30–F39)
3. Neurosis, anxiety state, obsessional state, depressive reaction (ICD–10, F40–48)
4. Personality disorders, alcoholism, drug misuse (ICD–10, F60–F69)
5. Organic disorder (ICD–10, F00–F09)

6. Diagnosis not given, no psychiatric diagnosis.

Overall 26% had schizophrenia, 36% affective illness, 10% neurosis and 14% personality disorders.

There were significant differences between the sexes. Of the males 31% had schizophrenia (women 17%), 29% affective illness (47% women), 9% neurosis (13% women) and 18% personality disorder (7% women) (Table 11).

Previous contact with specialist psychiatric care

It was very common to find that individuals in our study had been involved in psychiatric care prior to the episode preceding the suicide, and many among them had been in-patients.

Of the out-patient suicide group 107 (70%) were reported as having had earlier involvement and 87 (56%) had been in-patients. Although 30% of the group had been admitted only once, the range was considerable, and as many as 22% had been admitted on five occasions or more, including a few with more than 20 admissions.

The same pattern was seen in the in-patient group, where 44 (83%) were shown as having previous contact. All of these patients had been in-patients, and admissions ranged from one or two admissions (20%) to 5 to 14 admissions (42%).

The previous contacts with specialist services among the discharged patients were rather less at 12 (36%). All but two of these patients had been in-patients at some time.

We enquired about earlier contact with social services and found that 92 (38%) individuals had been provided with specialist social work contact at some stage prior to the recent episode.

Earlier episodes of aggression or self-harm

Previous self-harm was reported in around half the total cases and some degree of aggressive behaviour was not uncommon (32%). Most of those showing aggressive behaviour had also shown previous self-harm (Table 12).

Physical illness

Physical illness was reported in 67 (28%) patients but this ranged widely from chronic conditions such as asthma or hypertension to more immediate conditions such as cancer. Men were twice as likely as women to have a physical illness.

Family illness

A family history of suicide was given in 25 cases (11%).

Circumstances immediately preceding the suicide

Clinical notes

Because of concern that the clinical team might have had limited access to previous details of suicide ideation or attempted suicide, we asked our respondents if previous clinical notes had been made available to them. The majority informed us that the earlier clinical notes from other teams or hospitals had been provided. **However among the out-patient group 31 (20%) responses indicated that clinical notes were unavailable.**

Awaiting admission to in-patient care

It was a matter of considerable importance to discover whether there were those amongst our cases who should have been admitted to hospital but for whom no bed was available. In only one case among the 154 out-patients was the patient awaiting a bed at the time of death. However, the lack of suitable accommodation in hospital and in community placements was raised by some respondents (see **Review of individual comments and observations**, pages 38–45).

Admission to in-patient care during recent episode of illness

Of the 154 out-patients 61 (39%) had been in-patients earlier in the episode of illness leading up to the suicide. It might be expected that this latter group would have had access to suitable community care on their discharge from hospital.

Detention Under the Mental Health Act 1983

Evidently the Mental Health Act had not been seen as relevant in the treatment of most of those out-patients in our study. In 18 out-patients it was reported that there had been detention earlier in the episode of illness, but only one was subject to Mental Health Act restrictions at the time of death. Among in-patients, however, there were 14 (26%) cases where the patient was still detained at the time of death. In future, such cases could usefully be looked at in more detail.

Care Programme Approach

We sought information on whether a care plan, as required by the Department of Health's Circular[7], had been instituted, and whether a key worker could be identified.

For in-patients we asked whether the patient had been subject to the Care Programme Approach. Of the 53 cases, 29 (55%) confirmed that this approach had been followed.

Among the 134 out-patients where information was made available there seemed to be only five cases where there was inconsistency among the responses of the team about the presence of a care plan. This may be due to a lack of agreement about what constitutes a care plan, but this is a tiny minority of cases and we do not regard it as significant.

Forty-four (29%) of these cases had been provided with a care plan. In 30 of these cases the plan was said to be operational. Curiously, there were seven cases where individuals were reported as not having a care plan but respondents indicated that a care plan was operational. This illustrates a little confusion amongst some staff about the operation of a care plan. In 82 (53%) of the cases a key worker was indicated, perhaps showing that care was being provided at a higher level than indicated by the reported presence of a care plan.

Of the 54 out-patients who had received in-patient care earlier in this episode, 22 (40%) had a care plan whereas 32 did not. Of the 80 patients who had not received in-patient care, 60 (75%) did not have a care plan, perhaps indicating that in-patient care tends to promote preparation of a care plan, whereas this is less likely if there is no in-patient episode.

Twenty responses about the availability of a care plan were received for the 33 discharged patients. Eight (40%) of the 20 had a care plan, whereas 12 did not. Again, with much smaller numbers, there was a tendency for a care plan to be in place if the patient had received in-patient care earlier in the episode.

We asked about the presence of key workers. Table 13 shows the professional background of the key workers in the 85 (35%) instances where this information was given.

Stage of assessment

The majority of cases were well-known to staff and very few were still at an early stage of assessment. Ten of the in-patients came into this category of well-known patients, while among out-patients eight had recently been discharged from in-patient care. It is interesting to note that 15 of the out-patients had reached such an advanced stage of treatment that they were shortly to be discharged back to general practitioner support.

Suicidal intent

Many of those in this study had a previous history of mental illness and self-harm. In addition, there was evidence of suicidal intent during the episode of illness prior to death. One hundred and twenty-four (52%) among the out-patients and in-patients had given clear intention of suicidal intent at some stage during this period.

Actions taken in response to risk of self-harm

In most cases where suicidal intent had been shown the staff had felt that the danger had receded before the death, and it was no longer necessary to continue with the measures such as increased supervision, change in medication and admission to in-patient care which had been put in place at an earlier stage of the illness. Continuing fluctuation in the patient's mood, however, made assessment difficult.

We were not able to gauge from the replies received whether increased observation had involved increased interaction with the patient on a one-to-one basis, but we noted that attempts to help the patient were reported as being complicated by the patient's lack of cooperation in a number of instances.

Significant life events

We asked for information about any events which might have had significance for the patient in the period before the death. There might have been incidents involving interactions with other patients, especially among those who were in-patients or attending day-units, or incidents involving family relationships, or social or employment difficulties. In a later section, a more comprehensive picture is provided by our respondents in their personal comments, but Table 14 shows the number of responses made in the body of the questionnaire.

The most common problems cited were "loss of self-esteem" and "break-up in relationships".

Capacity for relationships

Among in-patients, almost half of the group did not have any significant relationship with members of staff and a greater number appeared to be solitary and not to have relationships with other patients. At the other end of the spectrum, it was reported that among patients who had been able to form a good contact with a member of staff, eight of them were without this support, by reason of staff holidays or transfer, in the period before the death.

The patient's lifestyle

The views of our respondents were sought on three particular issues: namely, frequent changes of job or residence, conflict with the law, and abuse of alcohol, drugs or solvents.

Thirty-eight per cent of patients were said to be unsettled in terms of changes of job and residence. Twenty-eight per cent were reported as having been in conflict with the law. Thirty-three per cent had been involved with misuse of alcohol, drugs or solvents. In each of these groups, no difference was found between in-patients, out-patients and discharged patients.

Unfortunately no comparisons are available with a wider population of mentally disordered people receiving psychiatric treatment.

Behaviour while under psychiatric care

A number of items on the questionnaire sought to identify characteristics which might be common among these patients. However it emerged that the characteristics asked about were seldom present at a high level, less than 10% being "nearly always" present. Because the items in this section represent a first attempt to identify traits which may be associated with suicidal patients, it is not possible yet to make comparisons with other populations.

Even without drawing statistically based conclusions, it is worth noting some of the characteristics which emerged. Irritability and aggression seemed higher among the male patients, while vulnerability and dependency seemed higher in females and among in-patients. Women had higher levels of depression and in-patients appeared sadder than out-patients. Unpredictability and alienation tended to appear among men more often than women.

In the future it should be possible to compare these findings with other groups of psychiatric patients and to discover if any particular grouping of characteristics is more common in the suicide groups.

Reaction to the patient

Respondents were asked to rate a number of statements about their own reaction to the patient. These statements were designed to investigate whether there had been any breakdown in the relationship between the patient and the clinical staff and also the feelings of the staff about the patient.

Mental health staff reported themselves as concerned and caring in the relationship with the patient, and only exceptionally did staff believe that there was an element of deliberate disability in the patient's symptomatology. Under 25% of raters indicated that they thought "often" or "nearly always" during the period of care that the patient might try to commit suicide. Equally, under 25% believed that the patient would not improve. Ninety-five per cent of the raters were of the opinion that the treatment offered was still relevant to the patient. This tends to indicate that suicidal outcome of the cases was unexpected to the staff who supplied the ratings.

The inter-correlations of the reactions of the clinical staff suggested a pattern of three dimensions of concern. The main dimension combined worries about patient's welfare, frustration at the progress of the case and frustration with the patient. Another dimension concerned the caring and empathic feelings that the clinical staff member had towards the patient. A final dimension roughly corresponded to issues concerning the patient's manipulation of their symptomatology. In future research it will be useful to develop such scales to see if suicidal patients reliably rate differently on these dimensions compared to other patient groups and whether such scores are helpful in alerting staff to the possibilities of problems in the care of the patient.

Cooperation with treatment plans

Among both in-patients and out-patients there had often been difficulties in maintaining a treatment programme, and this was usually because the patient did not wish to cooperate with the proposed plans. This had led on occasions to discussion among the psychiatric team about the possibility of formal detention. This was rarely initiated, however. The decision was affected by difference of professional opinion on only three occasions.

We asked about the success of arrangements for out-patient contact between patient and staff, and received responses in 130 (87%) cases. Follow-up arrangements were made for 96% of these patients, but in at least 24% of the cases difficulties developed in maintaining contact. In 27% of cases there were lapses in the taking of prescribed medication. Overall there were problems of clinical supervision in 40% of the out-patients. However it must be recognised that suicide still occurred among the 60% where no problems were noted.

The suicide event

Method

The differences in method of suicide found between the sexes and between in-patients, out-patients and discharged patients were noted in those 236 cases where an entry had been made in the questionnaires.

Jumping, hanging and poisoning were the three most common causes of death (Tables 15a–c). Hanging was the most frequent method of suicide in men, and poisoning the most common in women. Tables 16a and 16b show the method of suicide according to sex. It is of particular importance to clinicians to learn about the deaths of in-patients (Table 15a).

We asked whether the 53 in-patients had died in the hospital or at home or in some other place, and we also asked whether their absence from the hospital was with permission or without permission. The information available to us showed that only 14 of the in-patients died in hospital. Ten (19%) died in their home and 25 (47%) died in some other place. Of the 10 patients who died in their home, all had been on leave from the hospital at the time. Among those who died in other places, nine (36%) were on leave, and 12 (48%) were away from hospital without permission. Details were not available on the other patients, but we note that at least 35 of the 49 (71%) patients killed themselves while away from hospital.

It is of interest to clinicians to discover that among the 60 cases of self-poisoning only a small number (eight; 13%) were in-patients (Table 15a), but it would have been more useful to have had a complete record of the type of drug used.

Of 29 cases of jumping, 16 (55%) were in-patients at the time of death. Eleven cases were absent from the ward or on leave from hospital.

It is noteworthy that, in the case of both males and females, more than half of those who were in-patients committed suicide away from the hospital ward, when they had either been granted leave or had left the ward without the knowledge of hospital staff.

Among out-patients, easy access to cars resulted in 13 (8%) deaths by car exhaust fumes, while none were reported among in-patients.

Coroners' verdicts

We asked whether there had been disagreements between the Coroner's formal verdict, and the clinician's view of whether death had resulted from a deliberate suicidal action. In a number of cases no verdict had yet been reached, but among all the deaths, there had been occasions where the Coroner's verdict had been accidental death/misadventure and was thus different from clinical opinion. This is in keeping with our information from Coroners that suicide is recorded only where there is clear-cut evidence of intent.

Review following the death

The extent to which there was a formal staff review following the death depended very much on individual circumstances and on the number of staff members involved in care.

Some patients had only been seen on one occasion for assessment by one member of the psychiatric team and no staff review was initiated. At other times as many as five or six staff came together to share their experiences of coping with the care of the patient and with the death. Occasionally the family doctor was involved in this meeting. For in-patients, the review took place very soon after the death and was carried out in all but four cases. Reviews for out-patients were less frequent (97 cases) and took place in the month following death.

Review of individual comments and observations

We looked on individual observations as being just as valuable as the structured responses to the questionnaires. Each questionnaire was read carefully and the written comments extracted in such a way that there was no serious overlap or duplication between respondents dealing with the same cases. Comments were listed under the following six headings: Clinical management and staff responsibilities; Protocols and guidelines; Family involvement; Important life events for patient before death; Recommendations following review; Compliance with treatment.

Clinical management and staff responsibility (168 comments)

As with homicides, it is evident that in many cases the suicide had come as a complete surprise to the clinical team. The patient was well-known to team members, perhaps over many years, or was someone who had never voiced any thoughts of suicide or who had been closely monitored. Comments include: "unexpected by me and by his relatives"; "had just been assessed by duty doctor, by qualified nurse and by community support worker"; "routinely checked for suicidal ideation on day before suicide and known to the service for twenty years"; "There was no way of preventing the suicide of this intelligent person who was aware of the long-term consequences of the illness" or "After great deliberation, I consider there are no ways in which the likelihood of suicide could have been prevented".

A theme which recurred fairly frequently was the association between the death and some change in care. A member of staff was absent – "his favourite nurse was on community placement" or "his own consultant was on holiday at the time". A move to another ward might be imminent or discharge from hospital had just occurred – "he died four days after discharge and before out-patient care had been arranged".

Problems related to the attitude and behaviour of the patient are more frequently mentioned under **Compliance with treatment** (page 45), but are also reported under this section – "after an overdose, had discharged herself from a General Hospital Unit and could not be contacted"; "he dived through a window. Nursing staff were beside him at the time".

Possible deficiencies in the clinical care of the patient were discussed by our respondents – "perhaps there should have been an in-depth assessment prior to discharge"; "more frequent psychotherapeutic interviews should have been provided"; "the consultant might have been informed of patient's failure to arrive for admission and could then have made a home visit"; "drugs should have been dispensed in smaller amounts and more frequently"; "the ward team should have been more insistent".

However, while acknowledging that a greater level of supervision might have helped, it was pointed out that a patient might often resent a too intrusive intervention. "More close observation was not warranted"; "At the insistence of the patient, contact was made only by telephone"; "The patient had failed to attend and had not been re-contacted".

More general difficulties in providing proper care for the patient were described. The layout of a residential home for mentally ill people was such that staff levels were inadequate to allow effective supervision. Patients with long term problems did not have access to appropriate placements in the community – "no day hospital and no community mental health centre"; "stuck in hospital because no community placements available"; "a patient was left in an unsupervised unobserved single room for several hours"; "no beds were available"; "had moved to a Dispersed Hostel Scheme where intensive support was provided by non-resident staff". In a number of cases it was reported that patients were being nursed in intensive care units which were full or over-full and where there were many patients requiring intensive care which simply could not be provided in that setting. "Staff level low due to sickness – agency nurses inadequate".

On staffing, we received a number of disturbing comments. In the community, staff working in hostels were "young and untrained": "CPN had not been able to take up the case"; "supervision by social worker was inadequate because of burden of comprehensive assessment forms". It was pointed out to us that supervision in an inner city community was particularly difficult – "Many patients default as they begin to improve; while a CPN should visit defaulting patients, this would be totally beyond realistic resources"; "If CPN had not been so overloaded she would have been able to offer him more support in his efforts to give up drinking".

Even when numbers of staff were said to be sufficient, there was sometimes concern about their ability to cope with the needs of the patient – "I wonder if more time and more training would have allowed the identification of suicidal intent". Self-questioning by our respondents about the appropriateness of the level of seniority and experience of staff dealing with the patient is a matter of considerable importance.

Training in the identification of people at risk is a recurring theme, particularly for volunteers and non-psychiatric staff in community services. More complicated, perhaps, is the concern that patients are being seen by junior members of staff – "interview by consultant as well as senior house officer, might have given greater confidence to the patient"; "Consultant should be more involved in giving instructions about supervision or leave, particularly for detained patients"; "It would have been evident to a more experienced clinician that this was a major risk"; "no appointment was available to see a counsellor"; "I wish the consultant had interviewed him alone"; "the nurse in charge was too inexperienced"; "On admission she had been assessed by a junior doctor and an enrolled nurse"; " the consultant was responsible for excessive numbers of elderly people and the CPN was on leave at the time of the death"; "Staff levels were cut back at the time".

Sometimes we sensed the uncertainty experienced by clinicians about the extent to which they should have been able to make a more direct intervention, yet realised that there were difficulties in taking a more positive approach. "Death could have been avoided only if there had been a great restriction on all the other patients"; "I felt instinctive concern, but unfortunately he was not sectionable"; "to transfer him to a secure unit would have been an over-reaction, but he did require consistent close observation"; "Intervention was difficult once patient had moved to a different GP and a different Trust".

Protocols and guidelines (71 comments)

In the questionnaire, we asked whether any code of practice was in place to cover the supervision of suicidal patients or any routine action to be taken in the event of a patient showing active suicidal behaviour or, in the case of an in-patient, leaving the ward. Comments indicating the use of the Mental Health Act *Code of Practice* or any other general guidance on good clinical practice were included under this heading. Some respondents indicated some general principles which were in place to deal with all patients rather than being specific to the death to which our questions referred.

There were only 80 positive responses to the item on the questionnaire: *Did the team have an agreed code of practice concerning the care of suicidal patients?*. Additional written comments described fairly standard and widely accepted measures dealing with patients at risk of harming themselves and those who left the hospital without the agreement of staff. It was not surprising to find that such guidelines were much clearer and more formalised for those who were in-patients.

For suicidal patients there was usually a system of actions to be taken to establish the level of supervision and observation required. This ranged from general observation to 24-hour one-to-one supervision by nursing staff. These actions varied from formal written policies to an informal recognition that a range of supervision was necessary. "Policy agreed by managers/nurses including close observation and one-to-one nursing"; "Level of observation decided by doctor and nurse on admission and whenever mental state warranted"; "All actively suicidal patients are transferred to high dependency ward"; "Policy held in ward manual".

For patients in the community, the importance of informing others of suicidal risks was very much in the minds of community staff. "Agreed procedure to inform GP, consultant and social services"; "increase monitoring and admit to day-care". In addition to increase of observation, the medication being prescribed would be reviewed routinely.

Family involvement (39 comments)

The role of the family, and its involvement in the treatment plan, were sometimes crucial elements in the care of the patient. Often the clinical staff were able to point to the support given to the patient by family and friends. Occasionally difficulties were reported which had complicated the patient's treatment and might have been related to the patient's decision to commit suicide. It is these latter cases, dealing with interaction between patients and their families and also between families and staff, which are included under this heading.

Conflict within the family was mentioned in a number of responses, and failure by family members to keep in touch with the patient, particularly while an in-patient and particularly on special occasions such as birthdays, was seen as a precipitant of a suicide. It is perhaps not surprising, given public attitudes to mental health problems, that people who are suddenly faced with mental illness in their own family are at a loss as to how they should react. Sometimes they become over-anxious and try to control the treatment arrangements – "insisted that he should be allowed to leave the ward to attend the OT Department; he disappeared on the way"; "his controlling wife persuaded him to refuse ECT". Often they refuse to accept the recommendations of the medical staff – for in-patient care, or for a particular treatment, or for detention under the Mental Health Act 1983.

Where a patient refuses to allow contact by staff with the family this can lead to considerable misunderstandings, but there were frequent occasions when families were contacted with the full agreement of the patient and failed to respond to the invitation to meet members of staff – "family failed all appointments given to them" ; "family refused to see social worker and would not make an appointment with the consultant".

On a number of occasions it is suggested that it must have been fairly obvious to the family that someone was suicidal, but, with misplaced loyalty or denial of the possibility, they took no action to alert staff to their fears. "Very rarely contacted us to express their concern"; "husband failed to report his wife's very serious suicide attempt only ten days before her death".

Even when families were in regular contact with the patient and with the clinical team, there was sometimes evident hostility towards those carrying out the treatment – "family frequently threatening towards nursing staff"; "family very anti-psychiatry".

Important life events for patient before death (146 comments)

We asked about events occurring during this period of psychiatric care which might have been of particular significance to the patient. Frequency of these events were shown in Table 14, but it was of interest to examine the nature of the events, as described by our informants.

The personal comments, numbering 146, can be sub-divided into the following areas: Relationships; Employment; Finance; Social problems; Bereavement; Physical illness; Alcohol and substance abuse; Retirement; Psychiatric services.

Relationships (55 comments). Under this heading are included all the comments dealing with relationships which were in peril, or which had broken up, or which appeared to put excessive pressure on the patient.

Most common of all was the breakdown of a marriage or partnership – "wife had left him"; or "discovered wife was having an affair and planned to leave him". Less commonly the pressure resulted from the consequences of difficult family interactions – "had been advised to move to a hostel away from his 'fraught' family". Occasionally pressures resulted from forced separation from children – "had opposed the compulsory adoption of her child through the social services" – or from serious illness in relatives.

Employment (17 comments). Loss of job, difficulty in finding work, and threats of redundancy and early retirement were included under this heading. Failure in an academic course or denial of a place in further education were also mentioned.

Finance (8 comments). Difficulty in coping financially was seen as an important event only occasionally – "delay in obtaining DSS benefits" or "owed money for drugs".

Social problems (26 comments). In a number of cases, stress prior to the suicide had been caused by a variety of situations which might be included under this heading – failure to be accepted for immigration, change to new address, criminal charges pending, or difficulties with neighbours.

Bereavement (12 comments). In 12 cases death of a close family member had occurred quite shortly before the suicide event. In one or two cases the death had been due to suicide. In other cases, especially in elderly patients, death had followed a long period of chronic ill health (nine instances).

Physical illness (9 comments). Among older patients there was sometimes an awareness of failing health or of a potentially fatal illness which was felt by our respondent to have been a factor in their decision to kill themselves – "this patient was becoming frail and was being considered for move to a nursing home".

Alcohol and substance abuse (2 comments). Misuse of drugs or alcohol was mentioned on only two occasions.

Retirement (3 comments). Unwanted or unfulfilling retirement was seen as important only in three cases.

Psychiatric services (14 comments). Events brought about by psychiatric intervention were sometimes seen as being unwitting possible precipitants of patients' deterioration. "She reacted to the direct challenging of her Munchausen behaviour"; "wife had taken a respite break"; "had just had an interview with the Employment Officer". Such interventions would be a normal part of clinical supervision of the patient.

Recommendations following review (126 comments)

We asked whether any staff review had followed the death and whether the circumstances of the death had led to any recommendation for change in the physical layout of ward (for in-patient care), supervision, treatment plans, communication between staff, admission arrangements, use of detention under the Mental Health Act 1983, and discharge from care arrangements. We also invited our respondents to suggest any other ways in which the likelihood of death might have been reduced.

The responses to these questions indicate some of the practical changes which had resulted from local reviews and offer other ideas for improving the care of vulnerable patients.

When staff reviews had followed a death by suicide it had often been difficult to ensure that all relevant staff had been able to attend: family doctors and social workers had greatest difficulty in coming to a meeting.

In many reviews it was concluded that nothing could have reduced the likelihood of death, either because there had been no sign of likely danger – "Agitation had preceded an earlier attempt but was not present before the death. No other evidence of increased risk" – or because all practical measures of supervision were in place – "he was given enough attention, care and treatment but was determined to end his life" – or because the patient would not accept the treatment plan which was offered.

Difficulties in engaging the reluctant patient was a frequent theme, "... considerable heart searching by clinical staff as to whether they should have been more insistent that the patient should have accepted the need for supervision or for medication or the benefits of day care or in-patient care" – "there should have been stricter monitoring and insistence on in-patient admission". At the same time, it was recognised that greater pressure on the patient might have been counter-productive – "she had threatened suicide if admitted compulsorily" – or out of line with present policies – "we might have ridden roughshod over patient's right to choose, but this sits uneasily over the Patients' Charter, etc".

There were suggestions, however, of ways in which improvements might be made through:
- attention to ward layout,
- attention to unobserved exits

- attention to observation policy
- review of nursing cover.

For example, when a patient had been placed on 15-minute observation, the nurses were distracted by the needs of 12 other at-risk patients and one man requiring the urgent attention of two nurses.

Medical cover, too, came in for much comment. Consultant involvement in decision-making, particularly when a junior doctor with little experience of psychiatry was in disagreement with experienced nursing staff, was seen as important, as was the regular availability of senior staff – "Consultant was on leave – no consultant could be found to provide cover".

Communication between all members of the clinical team and also with the family doctor was the subject of comment. It was seen as important that the community psychiatric nurses or social workers should report back on findings of home-visits. Any evidence of suicidal ideation should be shared with other staff and be available in all case notes. Prescribing of drugs by family doctors could be unknown to psychiatric team – "Communications were bad and patient had managed to be on the list of two GPs, one of whom prescribed extensively despite pleas from the consultant".

Admission to general hospitals might have provided an opportunity for psychiatric contact – "this known psychiatric patient was admitted with an overdose, yet psychiatric team were informed neither of admission nor discharge".

There was frequent reference to the potential benefit of greater contact with the patient, either through the development of more day-time activities at day hospitals and day centres, or by more frequent visits by community psychiatric nurses or other key workers. The role of the community psychiatric nurse was often mentioned and the development of a 24-hour community psychiatric nurse service and 24-hour crisis team was advocated.

Additionally, more direct contact between the consultant and the patient might allow a more accurate assessment of mental state and of suicide risk. The importance of such contact when the patient is improving and becoming more independent was particularly indicated.

It was recognised that many of the review proposals required more resources – "unfortunately due to pressure of work I cannot follow up all these patients"; "not enough CPNs to cover sick leave"; "insufficient funding for a trial of clozapine"; "ideally, patient would be visited on a daily basis, but resources were not available"; "After a domiciliary visit, no bed was available and admission to an emergency bed in another unit was not justified. Arranged day-care but Bank Holiday intervened".

The need for greater training and support of all staff, including those untrained in psychiatric practice, was a recurring theme, and in more than one case mention was made of lowered efficiency in staff as a result of family pressures and academic pressures.

A number of other measures mentioned by individual respondents should be noted. "Take back from the patient all unused medication"; "Ensure that visiting staff have appropriate language skills"; "involve neighbours and friends and encourage them to contact clinical team if concerned"; "Reduce the present waiting time (12–14 weeks) for referral to counselling service".

Compliance with treatment (191 comments)

Frequent comments were made about the poor cooperation shown by patients, and the difficulty in maintaining contact with them. Often the problem was felt to result from the patient's personality, and mention was sometimes made of the characteristics of the patients which had made suicide more likely. They were often seen as solitary, isolated people, sometimes rigid and inflexible, who found it impossible to build up a relationship with members of staff. They might feel threatened by events in the world around them, or had reacted to their circumstances by the feeling that "there is nothing to live for". They might have talked openly about the possibility of suicide but would then refuse further examination of those feelings.

Their self-esteem might be low – "I'm no use to anyone, just a cabbage". They might have particular difficulties in coping with a family relationships or a problem with drug addiction.

However, in a few cases it was particularly pointed out that the patient had seemed stable and had not been considered at any risk of suicide – "well-known to staff and never seemed a suicide risk".

To the clinical team, by far the most common and worrying aspect of patient behaviour was what they saw as a refusal to accept help from the professional team. Patients would refuse to take medication – "very poor compliance with medication" – or to accept the offer of admission, or attendance as an out-patient. Despite efforts by staff, one patient "refused offers of all the help available, from in-patient, out-patient, day patient or CPN follow up". Even if they accepted a particular form of treatment, they then did not turn up for appointments, refused the CPN entry to the home, and disappeared from home if any attempts were made to visit.

Even in accepting some arrangements, there were patients who made the rules of how this contact would be maintained – "would accept visits from CPN, but not from psychiatrist"; or "accepted visits as long as parents were not contacted". Staff clearly found situations like this very frustrating – "he could have been helped if he had worked more closely with the Mental Health Team" – "She wouldn't accept the invitation to come to the day hospital"; "Didn't reply to a letter offering counselling"; "refused to answer the door or telephone and would not accept voluntary admission".

What emerges from these responses is that in an appreciable number of cases staff have difficulty in engaging patients who are solitary or non-cooperative. In other cases, even where patients had taken part in a treatment programme, this had broken down, resulting in the withdrawal of the patient. The responses demonstrate the frustration of staff when they feel that they are not allowed by the patient to give their professional help. **Consideration must also be given to the possibility that services on offer may not be serving patients' needs or wants or have sufficient flexibility in their delivery.**

45

III Suicides – Scotland

We were invited by the Chief Medical Officer at the Scottish Office to extend the Confidential Inquiry to Scotland. The numbers of homicides by individuals who at the time of the offence were receiving psychiatric treatment is so small that individual inquiries should fully explore the circumstances of each case. It was of considerable interest, however, to discover whether there were differences in the pattern of suicides between England and Scotland. Scotland has different mental health legislation (the Mental Health Act (Scotland) 1984) and a different pattern of mental health services.

Identification of 49 cases in Scotland has been accomplished by direct contact with Scottish consultant psychiatrists who were informed about the Confidential Inquiry through the Scottish Division, Royal College of Psychiatrists. They received a personal letter from the Director of the Inquiry explaining the objectives of the Inquiry and inviting their participation. Reporting of suicides falling within the remit of the Inquiry began in August 1994; in 28 cases full details were known by the end of April 1995 but case collection still continues with 104 cases notified by 1st November 1995.

It must be emphasised that direct comparisons between the number of cases in England and in Scotland cannot be made as long as a comprehensive reporting of cases cannot be guaranteed.

It has been traditional in Scotland that suicides by people detained under the Mental Health Act, and by those who were in-patients at the time of death, should be reported to the Mental Welfare Commission. In addition to these cases, the Commission is encouraging clinicians to report suicides among other mentally disordered people known to the specialist psychiatric services. After discussion with representatives of the Mental Welfare Commission and the Scottish Division, Royal College of Psychiatrists, it was decided that the purpose of the Confidential Inquiry would be met best by having direct links between clinicians and the Director of the Inquiry, rather than by making use of information received by the Mental Welfare Commission.

This Report includes details of the **28** cases where complete details were received by 31st April 1995. Eight (28%) were in-patients, 15 (54%) were out-patients and five (18%) were discharged patients.

Demographic description

Sex
20 patients were male and eight were female.

Age distribution
21 patients were under 50 years old (Table 17).

Marital status
It was reported that 11 (39%) of the patients were single. Six were married or cohabiting, and a further six were separated.

Employment
The number unemployed (including those unemployed through chronic ill health) was 18 (64%). Only four patients out of the 28 were in employment at time of death.

Ethnic group
None of these cases came from ethnic minority groups.

Accommodation
Of the patients living in the community, four were accommodated in their own home with others, nine were at home alone and one was in hostel accommodation. No information was available on the one remaining patient.

Psychiatric and social background

Diagnosis
The spread of reported diagnostic categories among in-patients, out-patients and discharged patients is shown in Table 18.

Previous contact with specialist psychiatric care
Seventeen patients (60%) had previously received psychiatric care and, of these, 16 had been in-patients.

Details of the numbers of previous admissions were given in 12 cases: these ranged from 1–3 admissions (nine cases) to 4–7 admissions (three cases).

We enquired about social work supervision and it was reported that in eight cases there had been previous contact with social workers.

Earlier episodes of aggression or self-harm
Previous self-harm was reported in 12 instances. Episodes of earlier aggressive behaviour were also reported in 12 cases.

Physical illness
Physical illness was reported in four cases.

Family illness
In two cases, there was a known family history of suicide.

Circumstances immediately preceding the suicide

Clinical notes
Notes were reported as being available in 16 cases.

Awaiting admission to in-patient care
Among the 15 out-patients, one was waiting for an in-patient place.

Admission to in-patient care during this episode of illness
Eight of the 15 out-patients had received in-patient care earlier in the episode.

Detention under the Mental Health Act 1983
Three out-patients receiving in-patient care during this episode of illness had been detained under the Mental Health Act. One was still detained. Among the eight in-patients, two were detained at the time of death.

Care Programme Approach
In the case of five of the out-patients it was reported that a care plan was fully operational at the time of death. Seven of the 15 had been allocated key workers; the consultant being named on four occasions with a ward sister, a social worker, and a registrar each being given key worker status on one occasion.

Stage of assessment
The majority of cases had reached a stage of established treatment. Among the in-patients and out-patients, two patients were still being assessed. Treatment was recently commenced in three cases, well established in 10 cases, at a stage of rehabilitation in four cases, and pre-discharge in two cases. No report was available for two patients.

Alcohol or solvent abuse
It was known that four of the out-patient cases had taken alcohol before committing suicide.

Suicidal intent
Among in-patients, five had expressed suicidal intent during the recent episode of illness. All of these five patients had also expressed ideas of violence and aggression. Among out-patients, 10 had expressed suicidal intent and six of these had also expressed ideas of violence.

Actions taken in response to risk of self-harm
Only on three occasions was any mention made of actions taken once there was concern about suicide. In one case supervision was increased, and in two cases medication was reviewed.

Significant life events and relationships

Among in-patients, important events prior to death were noted on seven occasions. There were reports of 19 separate events for the out-patient group. Break-up in relationships or death of relatives were the most common disturbances.

Aspects of personality

Less than half the patients were said to have had a good relationship with members of staff, and for the majority there had been difficulty in relating to other people.

The suicide event

Method

The methods of suicide are shown in Table 19. As in the English cases, hanging is the most common method of suicide. Poisoning is the most common method among out-patients. Hanging was the only reported cause of death among the five discharged patients.

Among out-patients, four were living at home with other people and eight were living at home alone. Two patients were in other accommodation.

Among the eight in-patients, three died within the ward and one within the grounds of hospital. Three were at home and one was in another place. Only one of the patients was away from the ward without permission.

Review following the death

A review had been held in all the eight in-patient cases and seven of the 14 outpatient cases. Reviews had also taken place in the cases of all but one of the discharged patients.

Review of individual comments and observations

These were collected in the same way as described earlier in the report (pages 19–20) and were divided into the same groups.

Clinical management and staff responsibility (16 comments)

Comments about the relevance of clinical management were interesting, ranging widely over aspects of care. Supervising the patient was made difficult by insufficient nursing staff. It was also reported that supervision had sometimes been reduced because the patient was no longer thought to be suicidal or because the patient was not felt to be detainable under the Mental Health Act.

Code of practice (8 comments)

Most of these comments dealt with levels of observation and the need to notify different members of the clinical team (and the GP) about what levels had been agreed.

Family involvement (7 comments)

Adverse effects of marital discord, over-protective parents and estrangement from the family were noted.

Important life events for patient before death (24 comments)

Important events prior to the suicide included deaths of close family members, at least two being violent deaths, disturbance in close family relationships, loss of employment, and physical or mental illness among important contacts.

Recommendations following review (23 comments)

Several of our respondents felt that there was no way in which the death might have been avoided. In one example it was pointed out that the patient had been discharged from formal care after very careful review of circumstances, shortly before the suicide.

One case brought out the importance of close observation at a time when a patient was improving while receiving ECT. Another respondent emphasised the importance of trained staff in assessing suicide risk.

The value of using the Mental Health Act to detain someone was emphasised by two respondents. This was countered in another reply which suggested that if professionals had taken the risk of removing formal detention, a patient might have felt more optimistic about his future.

Compliance with treatment

Some patients made a decision to remove themselves from the treatment arrangements they were offered. Some strongly denied suicidal intentions.

Conclusion

Despite the difference in legislation and pattern of provision, there are no major differences between the findings from the Scottish questionnaires and the responses from England. Numerical comparisons must await a fully comprehensive reporting from both countries; in the meantime the Discussion section and the Conclusions in our report are equally relevant to Scotland.

IV Suicides – Northern Ireland

Shortly after we had begun to collect data for suicides among mentally ill patients in England we were told that a research project in Northern Ireland was examining all known cases of suicide in considerable depth[8]. Information about psychiatric history, including details of recent involvement in specialist treatment, would thus be available. The project supervisor, Professor Roy McClelland, and the researcher, Dr Tom Foster, offered to make contact with every consultant psychiatrist whose patient came within the remit of our Inquiry, and to send them a questionnaire accompanied by a letter explaining the nature of the Inquiry (Appendix 5). As with Scotland, Ireland is also subject to different mental health legislation (Mental Health [Northern Ireland] Order 1986).

As a result of this approach, 33 Northern Ireland questionnaires were returned to us. These covered 33 patients: 22 out-patients, three in-patients and eight discharged patients.

Demographic findings

Age distribution
Age distribution is shown in Table 20.

Marital status
Fourteen of the patients were single; 10 were married or cohabiting. The remainder were widowed, separated or divorced.

Ethnic groups
There were no ethnic minority groups represented in this sample.

Psychiatric and social background

Diagnosis
Among the 30 cases where a diagnosis was provided, eight patients were suffering from schizophrenia, ten from affective illnesses, seven from neurotic disorders and five from personality disorder (Table 21).

Previous contact with specialist psychiatric care
Details of earlier specialist treatment and of the circumstances prior to death were not always made available. However, it can be noted that at least 16 patients had

received earlier treatment, of whom 13 had been in-patients. Four patients had been in-patients on four or more occasions.

Earlier episodes of aggression or self-harm
Nineteen patients had been involved in earlier episodes of self-harm, and six of them in episodes of aggressive behaviour.

Circumstances immediately preceding the suicide

Detention under the Mental Health Act
Twelve patients had been treated as in-patients, three of them detained, earlier in the episode of illness leading up to their death.

Stage of assessment
Among the out-patients, 17 were already at a stage of established treatment and rehabilitation, but the three in-patients were still at the stage of assessment when they died.

Actions taken in response to risk of self-harm
In three cases consideration was given to increasing supervision for out-patients, or to admitting them to in-patient care, either informally or on a compulsory basis. Patients were not always willing to cooperate or to accept the proposals for this treatment.

Significant life events and relationships
Disturbed family relations were not uncommon prior to deaths, and the frequency with which patients experienced difficulty in relating to others (17 cases) was noted.

The suicide event

Method of suicide
Among all patients the most common cause of death was poisoning (10), followed by hanging (eight) and drowning (seven). See Table 22.

Review of individual comments and observations

From the 33 Irish questionnaires 83 personal comments were noted and allocated under six separate headings.

Clinical management and staff responsibility (4 comments)

All these comments related to the difficulties in providing close supervision of patients in the community with relatively low staffing levels.

Code of practice (10 comments)

Observation, increased to fit the needs of the patient, was described as the central necessity for depressed patients. It was stressed that guidelines should make clear the need for agreement on the place of close observation, policies on hospital admission and the importance of staff discussion.

Family involvement (5 comments)

Two families were reluctant to allow the patient to accept medical advice on appropriate care. On the other hand, one family could not be involved because the patient would not allow the clinical team to make contact.

Important life events for patient before death (25 comments)

The most common disturbance prior to the suicide was in the marital relationship, although break-up in friendships, conflict with the law, political concerns and illness of family members were also mentioned. Difficulties in dealing with the hospital environment and with the truculence of other patients was described in three cases.

Recommendations from review (26 comments)

It was seldom seen as likely that changes in clinical management would have prevented the death. Four comments emphasised that only long term "incarceration" would have removed the danger, and others expressed concern that more intensive supervision might have been counter-productive. The need for good exchange of information between different staff groups was noted and the value of more staff to provide interaction with the patient earlier in the illness was seen as more important than the numbers of staff around the patient at the time of death.

Compliance with treatment (13 comments)

Patients who were unwilling to stay in hospital, or who did not wish to attend as out-patients, or would not take medication were identified under this heading.

Conclusion

The responses from Northern Ireland were collected in a different way to those received from England and Scotland, but it was striking that the same circumstances were described and the same themes raised by our respondents. The Discussion, Conclusions and Recommendations in the present report are equally relevant to the cases of suicide by mentally ill people in Northern Ireland to which we had access.

V. Discussion

This Inquiry was set up with the purpose of pin-pointing any areas where a change in clinical management might reduce the likelihood of suicide or homicide by a mentally ill patient. Although we will not attempt to offer a blueprint for managing such cases, we have attempted to identify themes which might allow generalisation from individual cases.

This discussion is based on the Inquiry's findings, which are detailed in the previous section.

The discussion begins with a consideration of lessons from other inquiries before highlighting the key findings arising from the Inquiry.

Review of other Inquiries

It was of considerable interest, in preparing the *Report of the Confidential Inquiry into Homicides and Suicides*, to note some of the recommendations which emerge in the reports from the other Confidential Inquiries. Although the other Confidential Inquiries deal with entirely different areas of medicine, there is considerable overlap in the recommendations and conclusions, which include the need for:

- greater involvement of consultants
- more rapid communication between junior and senior medical staff
- greater attention to transfer of information when services are provided at more than one site
- improved information systems to identify cases
- more effective contact between all professional staff and with families
- training in the assessment and management of risk.

It was also of interest to look at the areas of concern which emerged in the local inquiries into deaths by homicide or suicide involving mentally ill or disordered people. These areas of concern are summarised below.

Hospital practice

- Delayed or inadequate discharge care
- Unsatisfactory follow-up after discharge
- Poor ward cover by junior medical staff
- Failure to maintain direct medical contact with the patient in the ward
- Lack of involvement of night nursing staff in day-time ward meetings
- Inadequate staff levels at weekends
- Unsatisfactory hospital policies in relation to:
     Leave of absence

54

Seclusion
Action following a serious incident
Admission and discharge
Contact with relatives

- Negative effects of mixing more and less disturbed people in one unit
- The repercussions of having no intensive care unit.

Community practice

- Loss of contact with psychiatric patients following discharge from in-patient care
- Failure to deal with non-attendance at clinics
- Unclear care plans
- Absence of criteria for seeking medical assistance
- Lack of expertise in rehabilitation.

General

- Unsatisfactory contact between senior management and consultant psychiatrist
- Poor inter-agency contacts and lack of joint working policies
- Lack of clear guidelines on observation and special supervision
- Inadequate hand-over arrangements
- Poor understanding of the use of the Mental Health Act 1983
- Insufficient secretarial staff.

The challenge for mental health services is to identify which of these recommendations are of relevance to individual psychiatric units, to bring them to the attention of staff and to see them acted upon.

The main themes which emerge from the Inquiry will now be discussed.

Demographic findings

The demographic findings in our two groups of homicide and suicide cases cannot be compared directly with other findings. Most studies of suicide deal with overall figures and are likely to include individuals with very different characteristics to our own sample. Our sample includes many people with long-standing psychiatric illnesses, and with features more in common with other seriously mentally ill people than with the wider suicide population. However, trends in suicide can usefully be examined and compared with our own results[9]. In the future it will be of interest to discover whether there are any significant changes over time in the make-up of the population being studied.

We had wondered whether there might be differences between the in-patient, out-patient and discharged groups in our study but statistical analysis of the data shows no differences. For most purposes, therefore, these groups can be dealt with together.

Similarities between suicide and homicide

Self-injury and aggression to others are frequently found together in the same patients. It is evident that the needs of both groups are very similar to each other and to the needs of other people with mental illnesses and mental disorders.

The multi-disciplinary team

Many of the patients studied in the Inquiry had been in contact with only one professional, often the consultant psychiatrist. However, the number of occasions on which two or more questionnaires were received (135; 56%) gives an indication of the active participation of the multi-disciplinary team. Community psychiatric nurses are given a prominent position as the most frequently mentioned key workers.

Any expectations that there would be widespread differences of opinion among members of multi-disciplinary teams were not borne out in the responses to the questionnaires. Differences were acknowledged in only a very few instances. In two cases, one a homicide and one a suicide, the likelihood of the death would have been reduced if a different viewpoint had been accepted.

Communication

It is striking that problems in communication feature so frequently in the cases reported to us and in the recent reports following individual cases of homicide. Not only are mental health professionals supposed to be replete with communication skills, but the topic has been prominent in medical publications in recent years, and central to management courses attended by clinical staff.

From the responses to our questionnaires, however, we sense that the presence of guidelines or codes of practice or care plans does not necessarily ensure that members of staff understand the instructions which they are given. Examples of misunderstandings are to be found in:

- the way in which potentially suicidal patients are supervised
- the arrangement for leave or discharge from in-patient care
- the transfer of care from one specialist team to another
- the transfer to primary care.

We may offer various hypotheses to explain these cases where communication has been deficient. In the older days of institutional care, there was a demand for ritual control of patients – seclusion to deal with aggression, suicide caution cards to deal with potential suicide. The move towards informality was accompanied by a more relaxed attitude among staff. This attitude was beneficial to direct patient care but perhaps encouraged a more casual attitude towards detailed and routine tasks.

The independence of each professional group in the multi-disciplinary team also means that certain items of information are seen as irrelevant to other professions.

The most popular hypothesis to explain poor communication, however, is that shortage of time leads to corner-cutting and reduced attention to routine tasks.

Perhaps the situation has been aggravated over the last few years by the rapid changes of personnel to deal with new tasks and new strategies within the NHS. This time of transition may be followed by the re-emergence of clear lines of communication between individual members of staff.

Care plans

Responses to questions on the provision of a care plan indicated that formal care plans had been established only in a minority of cases. However, in many other cases the informal equivalent of a key worker or care plan had been put in place.

When the Care Programme Approach was introduced there was some confusion among clinicians about how and to whom it should be applied, and who should initiate it. *Making Care Plans Work*[10] is an encouragement to clinicians to recognise that good clinical practice already requires them to set out a plan for the further care of their patient.

Ethnic groups

In the very small sample of homicides involving men suffering from schizophrenia (13), there were five involving individuals of Black Caribbean or Black African origin. Further investigation is required to discover whether this pattern continues. If so, the effectiveness of the present treatment approach for these patients must be examined.

Among suicide cases, the proportion of ethnic minority patients is rather larger than might be expected from the national population. It will be important to investigate the possibility that there are certain women from certain ethnic minorities who are not being referred and who then kill themselves in greater numbers than expected. Alternatively it is possible that family support and care is such that suicide figures among certain ethnic groups are reduced.

Important events

We have gathered together a large number of events which preceded deaths by suicide. While it is impossible to know without a control group whether these events are more frequent than in other psychiatric patients, it is nevertheless worth taking note of events which seem to be particularly relevant. Breakdown of close personal relationships of the patient was the most commonly cited event.

Supervision in the community

We have not been able to examine in detail the progress of wider community care for mentally ill and mentally disordered people. However, we have been given instances where poor communication, or loss of contact with a patient living at home, may have contributed to a death through homicide or suicide.

In many of the cases reviewed, however, it was not possible to discover any change in approach to the patient's management which would have lessened the likelihood of death.

It has been pointed out by some of our respondents that the only way to avoid death would be to reinstate greater use of residential care and close supervision. To do this for all those who are potentially homicidal or suicidal would require the supervision, by an army of professional carers, of a huge number of people who would not go on to harm themselves or others. Even those most critical of the present style of psychiatric practice would be unlikely to champion such a course of action. Instead of considering such unrealistic solutions, the way forward surely requires effective supervision in properly staffed day or residential units which are, as far as possible, part of the community.

Contact with staff

The great majority of the individuals coming within the remit of our Inquiry had been in contact with a member of the clinical team shortly before death. We have no knowledge, however, about the quality of this contact with the patient and the extent of involvement of senior experienced staff. These issues deserve attention in future studies.

Even if we have no information from our enquiries about the extent to which individual staff members have been able to develop good rapport with the patients who go on to kill themselves or others, we note the occasions when deaths coincided with changes of staff or times when staff shortages made follow-up difficult.

In the wider context of general psychiatric practice, the difficulty in finding sufficient time to carry out the range of duties required is often apparent. Attempts have been made to identify the length of time required to carry out responsibly the duties of a consultant psychiatrist:

> The central importance of face-to-face contact with patients as a quality measure needs to be established. We should be moving towards standards of clinical care that define for in- and out-patients the minimum acceptable duration of face-to-face contact time with a psychiatrist and/or other staff[11].

For those patients who slip out of treatment and then kill themselves or others, it would be of interest to learn more about their face-to-face contact with staff, particularly with those acting as their key workers and with the consultant psychiatrists responsible for their care.

Staffing levels

Although we asked a number of specific questions in the questionnaires about staffing levels, particularly in relation to in-patient care, we were not entirely satisfied that we obtained clear answers. We were more struck by the concrete examples of staffing deficiencies presented under **Clinical management and staff responsibility** (pages 28, 39–40) and **Recommendations following review** (pages 29, 43–45).

Sufficient staffing at all levels and in all professional groups is of such fundamental importance to the satisfactory care of potentially suicidal or homicidal mentally ill people that staffing requirements must merit frequent review. Reviews should take account of higher expectations regarding the quality of inter-action with patients.

Most in-patient units' staffing levels were apparently up to their agreed nurse complement. It is our experience, however, that agreed levels are often sufficient to cover basic patient care rather than offering an opportunity for therapeutic interaction between staff and patient. It seems unlikely that effective care can be given in acute wards with over 30 beds and with only three or four staff on duty.

For patients in the community it is still more difficult to decide on the adequacy of cover provided by all grades of staff. Even where a care plan is fully in place it does not follow that the time of contact between key worker and patient can be assumed to be adequate.

Staff training

All staff working with severely mentally ill people require initial training, and continuing education until they retire. These training levels should not be the prerogative of any one profession. It should also be a requirement that staff have appropriate knowledge about mental illnesses and their signs and symptoms, and about the characteristics of mentally ill people. Communication skills should also be taught. Staff should know something about the range of treatments available, both physical and psychological, and their efficacy.

All mental health professionals also need to know about procedures and legislation such as the Mental Health Act 1983 and the Care Programme Approach. Those employed in each agency need information about working practices and liaison with other agencies such as specialist NHS mental health services, social services, general practitioners and voluntary agencies.

Effective multi-disciplinary teamwork does not happen by chance. It requires encouragement by managers and active participation by each member of the team. Teams need continuing professional education, some of it involving the whole team together.

Strong leadership and good staff morale are seen as requirements for satisfactory services. More attention should be paid to these needs in staff training, especially in psychiatric training grades and consultant continuing professional development.

Additional support

We received little comment about the adequacy of supporting services available to the patients who came within the remit of the Inquiry, or about wider issues of housing and employment. By the nature of our sample, which includes many individuals with serious or chronic mental illnesses, it is not surprising to find high levels of unemployment. **Alternative daytime activities, however, are given little attention and deserve to be considered as an important aspect of patient care.**

Compliance with treatment

A striking proportion of the homicide and suicide cases were described as uncooperative, and failed to make use of the services offered to them. Some of these patients suffered from personality disorders, and some from problems of alcohol or drug dependency. Others were diagnosed as having a major psychiatric illness such as schizophrenia.

While it may be necessary to invoke legal powers to insist that such patients accept treatment, this is an area of great complexity which will be discussed below. It must also be asked whether the service being offered to some patients – crowded wards, unsuitable fellow patients, overworked staff – may not play an important part in leading them to distance themselves from the treatment they need. Many of these individuals have been assessed over a long period of time and are well known to the psychiatric service. It would often be inappropriate to deal with their lack of involvement in treatment by using statutory powers to insist on their cooperation. Nevertheless, we are left with an uncomfortable feeling that more strenuous efforts to insist on maintenance of contact might have been rewarded by fewer deaths.

Legislation

Most of those working in the mental health field understand the purpose of the Mental Health Act 1983, the powers of detention provided by the Act, and the new arrangements to allow for after-care and supervision of mentally disordered people. However, an opposing force to compulsory powers comes from the widely held view that psychiatric care should be on an informal voluntary basis for all, allowing patients to maintain wherever possible their autonomy and independence. Formal admissions to NHS facilities of patients detained under the Mental Health Act 1983 have increased by 31% from the years 1987–88 to 1992–3. Among those detained for assessment and treatment, including assessment in an emergency under Part II of the Act, the increase has been 38%. These figures represent episodes of detention and not the number of individuals detained.

It is our impression that the decision by the psychiatrist and the Approved Social Worker to use compulsion to ensure that a patient accepts psychiatric supervision and treatment remains an exceedingly difficult one, despite attempts to clarify the issues involved. The 1993–94 *Report of the Scottish Mental Welfare Commission* provides a good illustration:

> Although it is commendable to try wherever possible to maintain patients in their home environment, a combination of symptoms of mental disorder, reluctance to take medication or follow professional advice, and gradual social breakdown (which may include sexual disinhibition, threats, assaults, police involvement and eviction orders) should lead a doctor, psychiatrist or GP to give serious consideration to the application of ... the Mental Health (Scotland) Act [1984] in order to admit the patient to hospital.

Those responsible for the patient have to use their own experience, their own personal attitudes to paternalism and coercion and their awareness of the effect on the patient of admission as they "give serious consideration" to the application of the Act. If they err on the side of compulsion, then the appeal mechanism will ensure that inappropriately prolonged detention does not occur. To err on the side of laissez-faire, however, is less likely to be challenged, and may have fatal consequences.

We are in no way promoting a major increase in the use of the Mental Health Act 1983 as a way of reducing suicide or homicide. Nonetheless, we cannot help but notice the common but mistaken belief among some clinicians, held until very recently, that a mentally ill patient must be dangerous before compulsory detention is possible. **The Inquiry's findings indicate that there are situations where suicide or homicide has involved someone who might well have been detained, as the Act allows, in the interests of their own health and safety.**

It is worth reminding ourselves that the Mental Health Act deals with the compulsory care of individuals who are suffering from mental disorder "of a nature or degree which makes it appropriate for him to receive medical treatment in a hospital"; and "it is necessary for the health or safety of the patient or for the protection of other persons that he should receive such treatment and it cannot be provided unless he is detained under this section". There is no rule of thumb to be followed: only by frequent discussion with other experienced practitioners can the individual practitioner gain and retain an objective view of what action is most appropriate.

There are small groups of patients, well-known to their local psychiatric services, who regularly default from medication with the inevitable consequences of relapse. Where the patient has a serious psychotic illness associated with assaultative behaviour, it may well be appropriate for those supervising the patient to invoke legal powers to re-admit the patient to hospital.

Even when detention has been decided upon and put into effect, there remains uncertainty about the way in which a detained patient can be provided with supervision in an open ward. This, too, should be a matter for regular review with colleagues.

For some patients a legal power of supervision in the community may be beneficial. Unfortunately there remains disagreement on the best way forward in this area. The new legislation to improve the quality of care in the community (Mental Health [Patients in the Community] Act 1995) is seen by some as an anti-therapeutic community health law[12] and has led to differing views from clinicians. It remains to be seen whether the recent legislation and, in addition, the considerable Parliamentary interest in community care, will ultimately lead to a measurable improvement in the mental health of psychiatric patients.

Care in the community

In view of the continuing debates about the adequacy of care in the community, something should be said about homicide and suicide in relation to such care. It is factually correct to say that fewer psychiatric beds are available and that fewer psychiatrically ill people stay in hospital on a long-term basis. The degree of close observation previously available in a well-staffed psychiatric ward cannot be extended to the care of a patient living at home.

Some of our respondents replied to our enquiries about ways of reducing the likelihood of suicide or homicide by pointing out that the only way of ensuring the avoidance of such a death would be to keep someone in hospital for life. Such a retrogressive approach to psychiatric care would clearly be against the interests of thousands of individuals who are best cared for in their own accommodation rather than in even the highest quality hospital facilities; and it would also fail in its objective as some people kill themselves inside the hospital.

What must be looked for in this Inquiry, and indeed in every review of psychiatric services, is a consensus on:

- the appropriate level of care
- the appropriate quality of care
- the way in which risk can best be monitored
- the way of responding to such risk once recognised.

Family

Three distinct themes emerged from contact with the families of mentally ill people who had committed suicide.

Sometimes it was the view of the relatives that death had been a direct result of unsatisfactory practice. Examples included cases where the patient was allowed to leave the ward unaccompanied, or where large quantities of medication were prescribed, or insufficient time was given for listening to the patient.

Responses to our questionnaires indicated that clinical teams had achieved a high level of contact with relatives after the death. However, the suggestion was made that an interview after several months instead of in the aftermath of the death would have been more valuable. There were other families who had felt that support was lacking.

The most frequent complaint from families was that they were excluded from the treatment process. Parents wrote with great feeling of how they felt they were given no opportunity to meet the responsible doctor in order to express their own views about the illness, or to give information which might have been valuable, or to get some advice on what attitudes they should take to their disturbed child. Difficulty in gaining access to the consultant was also mentioned, together with dissatisfaction at the reliability of information gained from junior staff. Sometimes families felt that the staff were unaware of how ill and suicidal the patient had become. Others felt that they were given no advice about how to handle the situation at home, advice which they believed would certainly have been forthcoming if the patient had been suffering from a severe physical illness.

Evidently there are situations where families attempting to cope with a seriously mentally ill relative would gain relief by having their own personal support. We were impressed by the system of Family Support Workers developed by a voluntary organisation in north west England.

It is worth noting that staff sometimes felt that a family's failure to keep in close contact with the patient might have been a precipitant of suicide. In contrast, other cases were mentioned where staff felt sure that the family had been aware of strong suicidal intention, but that they had not alerted staff to the danger.

Resources

Although lack of resources was not often cited directly as a cause of disaster, many of the problems pointed out have resource implications. A few of these are worth highlighting:

- Poor quality of accommodation, whether in hospital or in the community, is seen as a predisposing factor to homicides and suicides.
- Insufficient staff to allow adequate levels of face to face contact between patients and staff of all disciplines.
- Training needs are repeatedly pointed out. This makes three demands on resources:

    Cost of the training itself

    Cost of travel and subsistence to obtain it

    The need to continue the clinical work in the absence of this member of staff.
- The need for better communication and liaison between staff of different disciplines necessarily erodes time for direct patient contact.
- High quality community work will usually be more expensive of time and money than similar work carried out in a hospital.

Because of these resource implications there is a need for clear directions from the NHS Executive, while health commissioners and providers need to work out how this affects local services.

The future of the Inquiry

With improved methods of data collection and audit in the future it is likely that the task of obtaining reliable numerical information will become more straightforward, and may be dealt with by non-clinical staff. In our view, however, there remains considerable value in maintaining the confidential pathway between clinicians and the Director of a continuing Inquiry in order to ascertain the opinions, aspirations and recognition of failure of clinicians.

VI. Conclusions and recommendations

In this report we can offer no universal remedy that would have prevented the individual personal tragedies reported to us. Each of them was a distinct event, often unexpected, and seldom resulting from a dramatic breakdown in arrangements for psychiatric care. **It is unrealistic to expect that every homicide or suicide is preventable.** This Inquiry acknowledges that, even where psychiatric care has been comprehensive, situations will arise which are beyond the control of the supervising professionals.

However, the Inquiry has allowed us to examine a range of factors which may work against the prevention of homicides and suicides by mentally ill people.

Many of these factors are also found among the many recommendations in reports of earlier inquiries into individual deaths. This leads us to the alarming conclusion that these individual reports make little lasting impact on services for mentally ill people. There would be value in developing a mechanism in each area to allow recommendations from such reports to be reviewed on an annual basis. This mechanism might identify any aspects of local practice and resources which should be improved.

It is tempting to view some matters as more relevant to doctors, some to nurses, some to managers and so on. On reflection, however, we conclude that every member of the mental health service should be aware of the problems facing their colleagues and should study the factors which complicate their decision-making. The skills of clinicians in assessing risk of suicide depend not only on satisfactory training and continuing education but also on the time available to speak to the patient, the environment in which the patient is seen and the professional support from other members of staff. Similarly, the response of patients to treatment depends not only on the attitude of all members of staff, but on other factors such as their availability, the environment in which they meet and the quality of community resources in the neighbourhood.

Specific conclusions and recommendations follow.

Accountability

Lines of accountability and medical responsibility are quite clear for psychiatric in-patients. The situation is much less clear out of hospital and there is often no clear demarcation of areas of responsibility between the consultant psychiatrist, the general practitioner, the key worker and personnel from other agencies either statutory or voluntary.

Recommendation:

There is a need to define the areas of accountability for different professions working with severely mentally ill people not resident in hospital. Each member of the clinical team should understand their personal responsibilities for carrying out a patient's care plan.

Failure to comply with treatment

Probably the most commonly stated cause of failure of continuing care was that treatment had been offered, but not accepted or continued. This applied both to the offer of care and follow up by a staff member and the prescription of medication. In some cases poor compliance could be blamed upon the underlying psychopathology, but in others there were extrinsic factors amenable to correction. Poor compliance is multifactorial in cause.

Recommendation:

Better rates of compliance are an indicator of improved services to severely mentally ill people. Poor compliance needs to be tackled at all levels: local provider management in terms of CPA and supervision register, commissioning authority in resources dedicated to care of the severely mentally ill, and Department of Health in legislation for vulnerable mentally ill people in the community and guidance on care.

Assessment of risk of injury to self or others

Assessment of risk of injury to self or others is particularly difficult, for there is often little to distinguish individuals at risk from the many other patients being seen. Risk assessment must be seen as an important part of training and should be supervised and encouraged by all the relevant training bodies.

All bodies responsible for training professionals who will work in the area of mental health should include the assessment of potential self-harm or violence in their curricula. In addition, voluntary services involved with the severely mentally ill need to alert volunteers to the potential risks and give them ready access to professional support.

The findings of the Inquiry demonstrate that the identification of patients at risk of committing homicide or of killing themselves is extremely difficult. Any improvements in the ability of clinicians to assess risk would be of major importance.

Recommendation:

Employing agencies should ensure that all staff coming into direct contact with severely mentally ill patients receive training in risk assessment including appropriate refresher courses.

Agencies responsible for training standards and programmes should ensure that training in risk assessment and risk management is readily available and is suited to individual's needs.

Staff numbers

There were some statements made that staff numbers were inadequate or work load of consultant or others excessive. However, more noteworthy are situations described where the clinician did not complain about the inadequacy of staffing that was obviously present. Some clinicians appear to have become inured to inadequate conditions of practice and do not complain through disillusionment.

Recommendation:

Adequate staffing levels are required, in all the mental health professions dealing with the severely mentally ill, especially psychiatrists both consultants and trainees, mental health nurses both in hospital and in the community and occupational therapists. In each District, more clinical psychologists should be working with the severely mentally ill.

Clinical skills

Skills in developing a rapport with people who are seriously mentally ill or mentally disordered require special training and considerable experience. Training requirement will differ according to profession and also previous experience. Continuing professional development is required for all fully trained and qualified staff.

Although it was evident that regular contact had been made with most patients prior to the death, we were concerned that the time for one-to-one contact, where skills in developing a therapeutic relationship and opportunity for listening to the patient might be used, were very limited.

Recommendations:

Audit programmes should address the extent and quality of direct staff:patient contact.

Specific training is required for those joining mental health professions and adequate continuing professional development for established practitioners.

The mental health team

We were disappointed to find little reference in responses to questionnaires to the activities of the multidisciplinary team. We were left with some doubts about the reality in practice of such teams. Many patients were in contact with only one individual member of staff.

There were also instances where disagreements between different members of staff from different mental health professions had occurred. This was clearly detrimental to the care of the mentally ill.

A further concern was the number of occasions when a decision about the patient's management – spending time away from the ward, or giving up attendance at a day-centre – was left to the staff member most immediately involved. In many cases the opinion of another experienced member of the team should have been obtained.

(In the case of a formally detained patient, the approval of the consultant psychiatrist as Responsible Medical Officer is necessary.)

Recommendation:

The Department of Health should make policies explicit and management in health trusts and social services departments should improve the functioning of mental health teams by ensuring that:

- there is adequate level of staffing, with individual responsibilities in the team being made explicit.
- the members of the team receive continuing education, some of it involving the whole team.
- they encourage multi-disciplinary team working and provide training in team-working.

Communication

The Inquiry received reports of breakdown in communication between:

- hospital teams and community teams
- members of clinical teams
- psychiatric teams and other community services
- specialist units and primary care provision.

Recommendation:

Services for mentally ill people outside hospital should incorporate adequate protocols on information exchange into their operational policies to ensure good communication between those working for different agencies: specialist mental health services, social services, general practitioners, voluntary organisations and the criminal justice system. Effective application of the Care Programme Approach and of the Discharge Guidance 'Building Bridges' should improve inter-agency working.

Detention in hospital and treatment without consent

We were made aware of the difficulties experienced by our respondents in deciding on the use of the Mental Health Act 1983 in the cases of patients who might well benefit from treatment but were unwilling to accept the advice being offered. We gained the impression that the knowledge of the legislation was not in doubt. Consultant psychiatrists and Approved Social Workers found themselves working in more isolation from other colleagues than in former times when faced with difficult clinical judgements. A second opinion can be invaluable, particularly for patients showing aggressive behaviour, where the expertise and facilities of a forensic psychiatrist could be made available. The interpretation of the clinical nuances of sections of the Mental Health Act also deserves discussion in a larger arena.

Recommendation:

All professional mental health staff should receive induction training and continuing education about clinical and ethical aspects of the Mental Health Act 1983 and other relevant legislation.

Local forensic psychiatric services should accept as one of their functions the provision of expertise, both in terms of advice and if necessary, facilities, for the care of disturbed and potentially violent patients in the care of Health Trust psychiatric services.

The therapeutic environment

The Inquiry found that many of the patients coming within its remit had lost contact with the psychiatric services, and looked at some of the reasons for this. Sometimes it seemed that patients were reacting against an environment or a service which they found unacceptable. Overcrowded wards, excessive disturbance, and unsuitable community facilities militated against participation in treatment.

Recommendation:

Health authorities and Social Services should collaborate to ensure provision of an adequate number of in-patient beds and an adequate range of accommodation for severely mentally ill people. Living conditions should be pleasant, comfortable and acceptable to the patient. A poor environment engenders low morale in staff and patients.

Families

We were made aware of difficulties experienced by staff in dealing with families and by families in dealing with staff. It was brought to our attention that relatives sometimes find themselves trying to support someone with serious mental disturbance while receiving little advice or information from the psychiatric team. More attention to and treatment for family aspects of the care of the severely mentally ill has been shown to reduce relapse. We acknowledge the need for professional staff to observe the degree of confidentiality imposed on them by their patient, but also note the missed opportunity for active family involvement.

Recommendation:

There is a need for much wider provision of family involvement and treatment in the care of seriously mentally ill people. This has important and particular clinical significance for the patients coming within the remit of this Inquiry.

Voluntary and statutory services in the community

Many of the patients were described as being lonely and unable to make friends. The absence of comment from our respondents about the support, statutory or voluntary, which might have been helpful to patients suggests that they had not seen such matters as relevant to the Inquiry. In retrospect we recognise that the availability of appropriate housing, of stimulating day activities or of contact with voluntary groups is of considerable significance.

Recommendation:

A range of local services should be available and should interact fully with the specialist psychiatric services. There is a need for much closer integration of NHS, social service and voluntary contribution locally.

Personality disorder

Even where the primary diagnosis is another psychiatric condition, comments by respondents that personality difficulties or disorder was also present highlight exceptional problems of management before death. There is continuing difference of opinion amongst general psychiatrists as to whether those with personality disorder are amenable to treatment outside forensic services.

Recommendation:

There is a need for more research into treatment of people with severe personality disorders. There should be teaching to all relevant mental health professions on validated methods of treatment.

Changes in situation and provision of care

Changes in the pattern of care are well recognised risk factors, especially for suicide: change of ward, discharge from in-patient status, change of key worker necessitated by resignation or holiday, and so on.

Recommendation:

Mental health professionals should recognise the risk associated with change and take extra precautions and provide extra supervision at such times. The patient may interpret the change as rejection and a response should be made to these concerns.

The Inquiry

It is our view that this Confidential Inquiry has opened up a valuable source of information about the events surrounding homicide and suicide among people being treated by the psychiatric service. With spreading awareness among clinicians about the role of the Inquiry, we believe that it can develop further as a source of knowledge drawing on personal clinical experience in parallel both with the more formal information available from national data collection and with the information gained through local audit.

The interest among clinicians around the country has been considerable. Individuals have indicated their wish to support the work of the Inquiry, while we find that the very act of completing the questionnaire and of responding to the many items included in it provides a useful stimulus to reappraisal of clinical practice.

Recommendation:

In the future development of the Inquiry, the opportunity for direct contact between clinicians and the Director of the Inquiry should be retained. The Confidential Inquiry should concentrate on issues which are difficult to elicit in local audit either through insufficient numbers or because of sensitivity through breach of confidentiality.

VII. Tables

Table 1. Homicide – Gender

Patient status	Male	Female
In–patients	2	0
Out–patients	24	12
Discharged	1	0
Total	27	12

Table 2. Homicide – Age Distribution

Patient status	Under 20	20–24	25–29	30–39	40–49	50–59	60–69	70 +	Not given
In-patients (M)	0	0	1	0	0	1	0	0	0
Out-patients (M)	3	2	6	3	3	3	1	0	3
Out-patients (F)	0	1	2	7	1	1	0	0	0
Discharged (M)	0	0	1	0	0	0	0	0	0
Total	3	3	10	10	4	5	1	0	3
%	7.7	7.7	25.6	25.6	10.3	12.8	2.6	0	7.7

Table 3. Homicide – Marital Status

Single	19
Married	7
Co-habiting	6
Separated	3
Divorced	3
Not known	1

Table 4. Homicide – Diagnosis

	Out-patient		In-Patient		Discharged	
	Male	Female	Male	Female	Male	Female
Schizophrenia and paranoid illness	12	1	2	0	1	0
Affective illness	5	9	0	0	0	0
Neurosis	0	0	0	0	0	0
Personality disorder	7	2	0	0	0	0
Organic disorder	0	0	0	0	0	0
Total	24	12	2	0	1	0
%	61.6	30.7	5.1	0	2.6	0

Table 5 a. Method of Homicide – All Cases

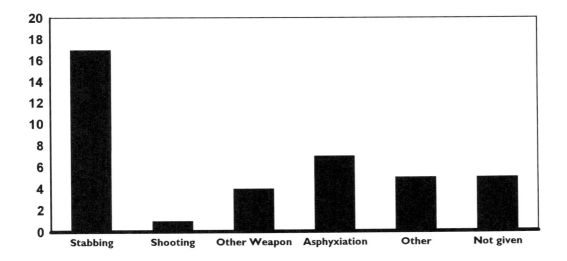

71

Table 5 b. Method of Homicide – Males

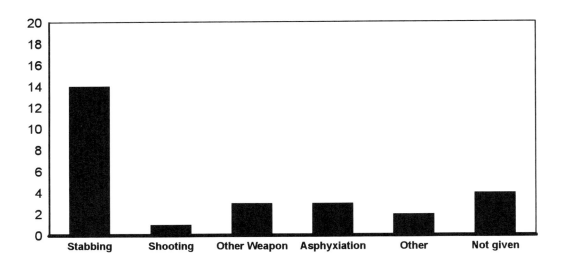

Table 5 c. Method of Homicide – Females

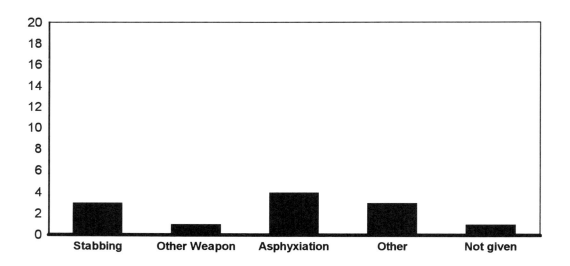

Table 6 a. Homicide – Victims of Male Patients

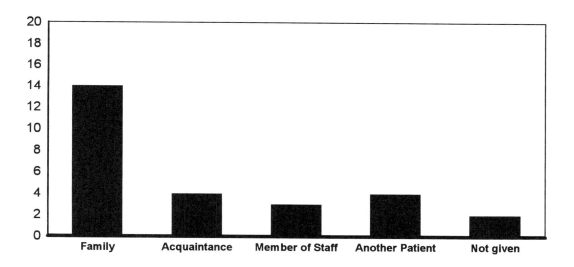

Table 6 b. Homicide – Victims of Female Patients

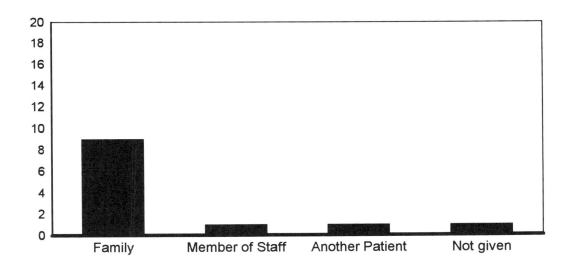

Table 7. Suicide, England – Questionnaires Returned

	1	2	3	4+
Out-patients	76	53	17	8
In-patients	4	27	11	11
Discharged patients	23	8	0	0

Table 8. Suicide, England – Gender Distribution by Percentage

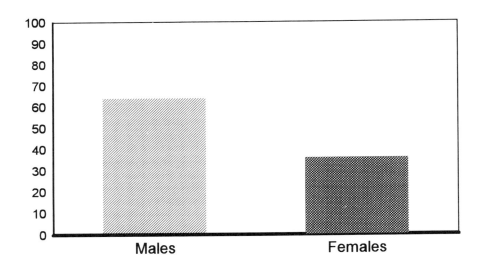

Table 9. Suicide, England – Age Distribution

Patient age	Male	Female	Total
Under 20	2	2	4 (1.6%)
20–24	14	8	22 (9.1%)
25–29	18	9	27 (11.6%)
30–39	31	9	40 (16.6%)
40–49	25	15	40 (16.6%)
50–59	23	11	34 (14.1%)
60–69	19	11	30 (12.5%)
70 +	11	13	24 (10%)
Not given	10	9	19 (7.9%)
Total	153	87	240 (100%)

Table 10. Suicide, England – Ethnic Representation

Caucasian	219
Black Caribbean	7
Black African	5
Black – Other	0
Indian	1
Pakistani	3
Bangladeshi	0
Chinese	1
Other	2
Not given	2
Total	240

Table 11. Suicide, England – Diagnosis

	Out-patient		In-Patients		Discharged	
	Male	Female	Male	Female	Male	Female
Schizophrenia and Paranoid illness	26	10	19	4	3	1
Affective illness	31	21	7	15	7	5
Neurosis	12	9	0	1	2	1
Personality disorder	22	3	0	1	5	2
Organic disorder	1	1	0	0	0	0
No diagnosis	13	5	4	2	5	2
Total	105	49	30	23	22	11
%	44	20	12.5	9.6	9.2	4.6

Table 12. Suicide, England – Episodes of Aggression or Self-harm

Patient status	Previous self-harm	Previous violent, aggressive behaviour
In-patients	31 (58%)	18 (34%)
Out-patients	72 (47%)	51 (33%)
Discharged	15 (45%)	10 (30%)

Table 13. Suicide, England – Professional Background of Key Worker

Consultant psychiatrist	28
Other medical staff	14
Nursing staff/ community psychiatric nurse	20
Psychologist	7
Social worker	8
Day centre worker	2
Other	6

Table 14. Suicide, England – Events and Relationships

Patient status	Events in treatment area	Events outside treatment area
In-patients	23 (43%)	29 (54%)
Out-patients	62 (40%)	67 (43%)
Discharged	5 (18%)	18 (54%)

Table 15 a. Suicide, England – Method of Suicide by In-patients

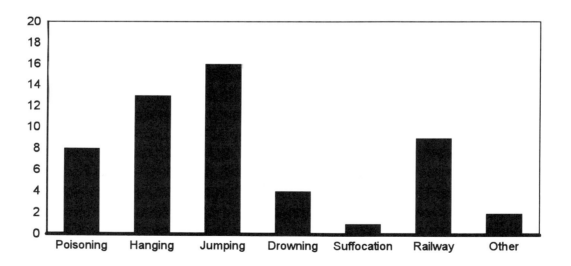

Table 15 b. Suicide, England – Method of Suicide by Out-patients

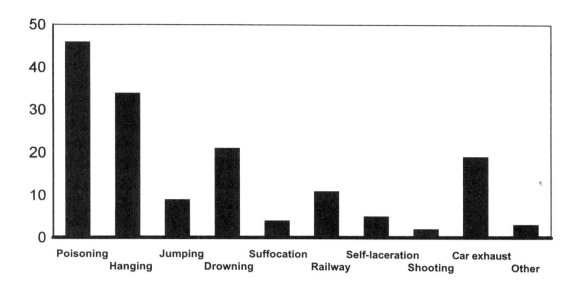

Table 15 c. Suicide, England – Method of Suicide by Discharged Patients

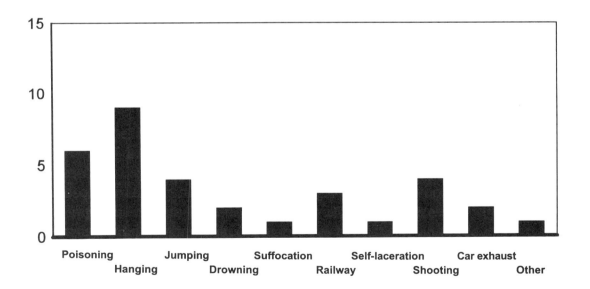

Table 16 a. Suicide, England – Method of Suicide in Males

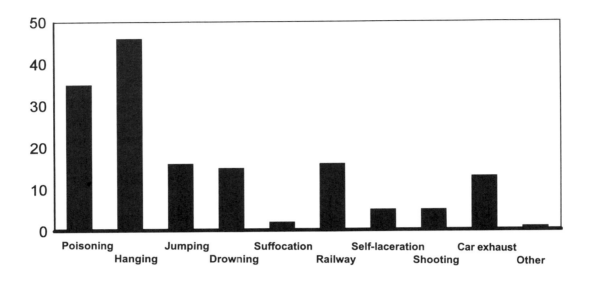

Table 16 b. Suicide, England – Method of Suicide in Females

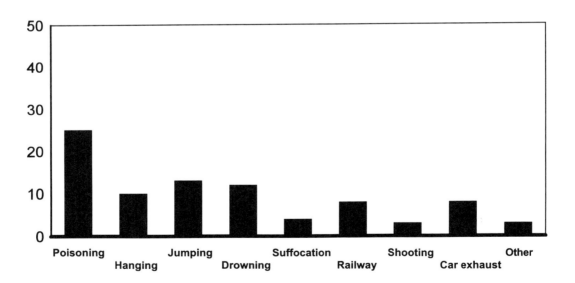

Table 17. Suicide, Scotland – Age Distribution

Patient status	Under 20	20–24	25–29	30–39	40–49	50–59	60–69	70 +	Not given
In-patients	0	0	3	1	0	1	2	1	0
Out-patients	0	0	1	4	4	2	1	0	3
Discharged	0	3	1	1	0	0	0	0	0
Total	0	3	5	6	4	3	3	1	3
%	0	10.7	17.9	21.4	14.3	10.7	10.7	3.6	10.7

Table 18. Suicide, Scotland – Diagnosis

Diagnosis	Out-patients	In-patients	Discharged patients	Total
Schizophrenia and paranoid illness	4	3	0	7
Affective illness	7	2	2	11
Neurosis	1	1	1	3
Personality disorder	2	1	1	4
Organic disorder	0	0	1	1
No diagnosis	1	1	0	2
Total	15	8	5	28

Table 19. Suicide, Scotland – Methods

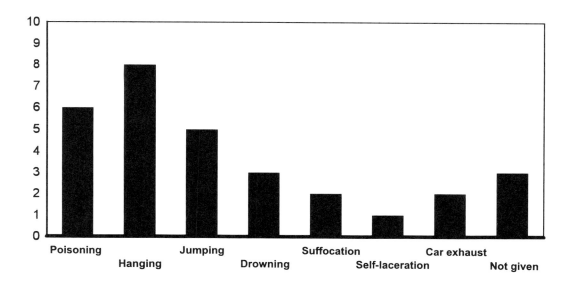

Table 20. Suicide, Ireland – Age Distribution

Patient status	Under 20	20–24	25–29	30–39	40–49	50–59	60–69	70 +	Not given
In-patients	0	2	0	1	0	0	0	0	0
Out-patients	0	1	2	3	4	2	4	3	3
Discharged	1	0	0	0	1	1	0	0	5
Total	1	3	2	4	5	3	4	3	8
%	3.0	9.33	6.01	12.0	15.0	9.33	12.0	9.33	24.0

Table 21. Suicide, Ireland – Diagnosis

Patient status	Out-patient	In-patient	Discharged patient	Total
Schizophrenia and paranoid illness	5	1	0	6
Affective illness	5	2	2	9
Neurosis	4	0	3	7
Personality disorder	4	0	2	6
Organic disorder	0	0	1	1
No diagnosis	4	0	0	4
Total	22	3	8	33

Table 22. Suicide, Ireland – Methods

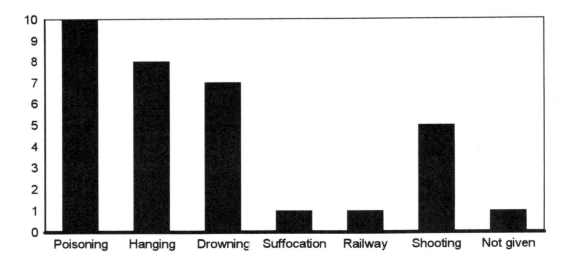

Appendix 1. An overview of homicide and suicide by mentally ill people

The Confidential Inquiry is concerned with homicides and suicides by people who are receiving specialist psychiatric treatment for mental illness or disorder. In order to place the Inquiry in context, it should be stressed that such deaths represent only a small proportion of the total number of deaths arising as a result of murder and suicide in society.

The aim of this appendix is to offer an overview of homicide and suicide and to highlight some of the wider issues which form a background to this study.

Homicide

The term homicide covers all unlawful killings and includes the offences of murder, manslaughter and infanticide. In Britain, homicide is an unusual event. The annual Criminal Statistics published by the Home Office (1994) record that there were between 450 and 500 annual convictions for homicide in England and Wales over the last decade. About 80% of those convicted were legally "normal". The "abnormal" homicides made up the remainder, including 70–80 people convicted of manslaughter on the grounds of diminished responsibility and 1–10 convicted of infanticide. Between 1–5 people annually are found insane or unfit to plead. In addition, the abnormal homicide group includes those who commit suicide after the killing, between 35–50 people a year. Just under half of those convicted of manslaughter on the grounds of diminished responsibility will receive hospital and restriction orders (sections 37 and 41 of the Mental Health Act 1983). Thus, of 500 homicide convictions a year, the number who are regarded as legally abnormal is less than 100, to which must be added the murder-suicides.

In common with the generality of crimes, homicide is committed mostly by men (9 out of 10 cases). The victim is known to the offender in nearly three-quarters of cases, and in half the cases the victim is a family member or lover. About 15% of all victims are children, those aged under one year forming the largest group. The most common method of killing in 1993 was with a sharp instrument (31%). Strangulation was the next most common method for female victims (27%), compared with hitting and kicking for males (21%). The next most common methods were the use of a blunt instrument (12%) and shooting (12%). Only a minority of homicides (5%) were motivated by theft or gain, but almost half were committed in circumstances of a quarrel, revenge or loss of temper. A significant number of victims may have a mental disorder.

A legal distinction is made between normal and abnormal homicides, based on the existence of mental abnormality. However the difference is not always clear-cut, and it is important to emphasise that for the great majority of both normal and abnormal homicides the motivation is similar. Intense emotional arousal in the setting of a disturbed interpersonal relationship, sometimes accompanied by disinhibition with alcohol or drugs, is a common feature of many homicides. The random killing of a stranger by a psychotic individual is a rare occurrence.

The significance of a psychiatric disorder in homicides will vary from case to case, and must always be viewed in the unique cultural, social and situational context in which every homicide occurs. In the category of abnormal homicides will be found the whole range of psychiatric disorders, including neurosis and personality disorder, learning disability, organic disorders and psychotic illnesses.

There is a small but significant increased risk of violence by mentally ill people, notably those with psychotic disorders, particularly schizophrenia. Much (but not all) of the violence perpetrated by those with schizophrenia is of a minor degree and homicide is uncommon. A detailed review of the psychiatric literature on violence and homicide by the mentally disordered is beyond the scope of this Inquiry. Readers are recommended the following publications, which contain relevant references: Monahan & Steadman (1994)[13] for an overview of violence and mental disorder; Bowden (1990)[14] for a review of the literature on homicide; and Häfner & Böker's[15] very comprehensive but rather dated study of abnormal homicides in East Germany (1973).

Häfner & Böker investigated 533 mentally disordered offenders who had killed or seriously injured over a 10-year period. The majority, of whom most were men, received a diagnosis of schizophrenia. They estimated the risk of a schizophrenic person committing a serious violent offence to be 5 in 10 000 of such offences. However, people with schizophrenia were one hundred times more likely to kill themselves than others. Violence in the schizophrenic group was associated with delusions with a content of persecution and jealousy, especially with delusionally experienced personal threat or harm. Men formed the largest part of this group and most of the victims were family members or involved in intimate relationships. A great majority of the group had been ill for more than a year and only a minority had received any psychiatric treatment during the six months before the killing. For those who had been admitted to hospital there was an increased risk of violence in the six months following discharge.

In contrast, the small group with an affective disorder contained a preponderance of women with severe endogenous depression whose victims were mostly their own children (a diagnosis of mania in those who kill is very rare). They were most likely to kill during the immediate post-discharge period when depressive inhibition had decreased. This group also included the majority of the murder–suicides in which the violence was part of an extended suicide. West (1965)[16] found that half his sample of murder–suicides were considered sufficiently abnormal to be regarded as insane or of diminished responsibility, had they been brought to trial. Two murder-suicides were referred to the Inquiry.

Among the group of mentally abnormal homicides are also those with a diagnosis of personality disorder, sometimes associated with substance misuse. Personality features may include, for example, immaturity and inadequacy, impulsivity and explosiveness, and over-sensitivity. The offence may occur in a setting of rejection or other threats to self-esteem, sometimes associated with transient disturbance of mood. These features may also be found to a greater or lesser extent in the normal homicide group. The degree of the "abnormality of mind" in terms of diminished responsibility (section 2 of the Homicide Act 1957) in such cases is often a matter of clinical and legal dispute. Yet this will determine whether the homicide is regarded as normal or abnormal. At the extreme end of the personality disorder spectrum is found the rare sadistic, and frequently sexual, homicide[17].

This brief review defines the small pool from which were drawn the cases which fulfilled the remit of the Inquiry. That is, cases which came within the group of mentally abnormal homicides and were also being supervised by the psychiatric services at the time of the homicide, or had been discharged from psychiatric care within the previous year.

Suicide

Over the centuries, society has been ambiguous in its attitudes to self-destruction, sometimes viewing it as a noble ending, sometimes as a sinful deed. Two of the best known characters in the Old Testament, Samson and Saul, killed themselves and apparently aroused no criticism for this action, while in ancient Rome it was accepted that suicide was a logical step for an individual to take in order to demonstrate loyalty to a friend, or to respect the wishes of the Emperor, or as a response to loss of dignity, shame or bodily suffering. Only in 17 of 923 such historical cases examined by Van Hooff was there evidence of mental illness and no blame or criticism was attached to any of those who had killed themselves.

The Christian revulsion to suicide continued from the second century right up to the present times and was supported by the civil law until the repeal of the Suicide Act in 1961. There were always those who wrote to defend or even support the personal choice involved in suicide and as we approach the end of the second millennium there is much concern about "the right to die", the use of "living wills" and the practise of euthanasia, the implications being that quality of life may be more important than mere prolongation of life. We mention these wider views only to point out that in this Inquiry we are dealing only with people who are mentally ill and who were receiving specialist psychiatric care prior to the death. Some mentally ill or mentally disordered people can make unimpaired judgements: however, the broadly held assumption is that their ability to make unemotional and objective judgements is likely to be impaired. It is therefore not appropriate to take a relaxed attitude to suicide within this group or to take the view that death by suicide is inevitable. The safety of people who are mentally ill or mentally disordered must remain a central issue for the psychiatric services, and the safe-keeping of those who are suicidal reflects the care which the service can provide for all the other patients under psychiatric care.

In considering the prevention of suicide, it is valuable to identify certain recognised risk factors such as previous attempts at suicide, recent relapse, isolation, alienation, recent discharge from hospital and certain demographic findings. In a review article on risk and prevention of suicide in psychiatric patients, Appleby points out that we must also take note of possible protective factors against suicide which are presently under-researched but "likely to lie in the nature of psychiatric care"[18]. It is, of course, the detail of delivery of care which is investigated in this Confidential Inquiry.

Many of the studies published on this topic are mentioned in the above review article, but one or two of particular relevance deserve mention. Studies by Barraclough[19], Morgan[20], and Crammer[21] focused on the deaths by suicide of psychiatric in-patients. Crammer particularly encouraged the idea of medical audit

> to test the efficiency of hospital management and the working of the medical nursing team. Suicide, which is not an intended outcome of treatment, represents an opportunity to review the way the staff are working together, using the equipment and building provided. Deficiencies in provision, in organisation or in training may be revealed.

Over the past decade the move to discharge patients from hospital and to treat them in the community, which had been slowly advancing over many years, took on a rapidly increasing momentum and raised concern about the risk of suicide among mentally ill patients outside hospital. A study in Oxford in 1993 showed that there is a significant clustering of suicides soon after discharge from psychiatric care. The patients studied had been short-term in-patients rather than long-stay patients who found themselves unable to cope with sudden transfer to the community[22].

Attempts to make a large scale epidemiological study of suicide by mentally ill people are bedeviled by a number of uncertainties. The national suicide rates come from Coroners' inquests, where the finding of suicide is rightly restricted to cases where the cause of death is indisputable. However, presumption of suicide can reasonably be made from the psychiatric history and from the circumstances of the death. Such cases are likely to be reported as an open verdict or even accidental death, yet their numbers add considerably to the true rate of suicide.

Turning to suicide deaths known to the psychiatric service, it might be thought that the psychiatrist responsible for the patient prior to death would have accurate information about the suicide, but this is far from common. Death outside hospital may never be reported back, especially if it occurs far from the catchment area or if the service provision is in a large city. One of the respondents to our Inquiry had discovered six recent cases of suicide by mentally ill patients known to the coroner but never brought to the attention of the responsible psychiatrist.

A further matter of interest is the extent to which the patients in our study can be described as "seriously mentally ill". *The Health of the Nation* proposes different targets for reduction in suicide rates, first for all suicides (15%) and then for those who are seriously mentally ill (30%). We have perhaps advanced a little from the situation more than a hundred years ago when Strahan wrote

> It is not likely that we shall ever get a definition of insanity which shall be so far reaching and, at the same time, so restricted and definite as to satisfy the various schools of thought: the legal, the medical and the metaphysical, and it is certain we shall never discover a means of getting to know the mental state of the suicide just anterior to his fatal act. It would seem impossible, then, that we can ever arrive at the stage where reliable statistics on the subject might be obtainable and it is clear that all existing statistics relative to the question are valueless[23].

Nonetheless, it remains difficult to define serious mental illness by diagnostic criteria, judging by the returns to our own questionnaires. We are content to take the view that people who are referred to the specialist psychiatric service are likely to be considered by their general practitioner as more seriously ill than those retained in their own practice.

It is not being over-optimistic to hope that in the future it will be possible to ensure that country-wide psychiatric audit, tied into other aspects of health audit, will ensure that accurate recordings of suicide will be available. For the moment, however, accurate epidemiological research into suicide among psychiatric patients must be confined to local tightly-controlled populations. A wider national inquiry, such as has been initiated by this Inquiry, must seek to do something rather different. The Inquiry offers an opportunity to identify a large number of cases falling within our remit and to use the comments from practitioners, given in strictest confidence, to build up a picture of the factors considered important in the individual cases. From these comments we can derive a number of themes which should be highlighted and fed back to those providing the specialist service.

The official returns of suicide are listed in the Coroner returns and show a fairly stable rate over the years, with a slight reduction in the numbers from 4242 in 1983 to 3740 in 1993. Deaths from accident and misadventure ranging from 11 827 in 1983 to 9273 in 1993 cannot give any indication of which of these deaths might be due to suicide.

Studies of deaths by suicide suggest that as many as 90% of people who kill themselves are mentally disordered[24] and it has been calculated that the lifetime risk of suicide for people with depressive illness is 15% and for those with schizophrenia 10%. Danger is greater in those who also misuse alcohol or drugs and those who also show personality traits of impulsiveness and irresponsibility. Social disadvantages such as having been in care during childhood, also predispose to suicide risk.

A controlled study of 5412 formerly hospitalised psychiatric patients found 68 deaths from suicide and 38 accidental deaths, these numbers being higher than a sex- and age-matched control group.

In spite of the gathering of detailed information such as this, the risk factors fail to provide sufficiently narrow criteria to allow practical predictors of risk. Some professionals suggest that attempts to reduce suicide rates at a national level are implausible and without scientific foundation. Others emphasise the importance of developing certain basic skills – a sympathetic ear, the offer of a dependable source of support, a quiet confidence without excessive reassurance and sometimes the ability simply to play for time. An attitude of fatalism – "It was bound to happen sometime" – is hardly in accord with the practical measures available to treat the crises of mental illness. Nonetheless, the psychiatric team wishing to offer support, medication, and temporary respite in a psychiatric in-patient or day patient unit is still faced on a daily basis with the decision whether and how far it is proper to interfere with the individual wishes of the patient.

The recent NHS management publication on prevention of suicide offers a positive view. The proposition that "suicide is not always preventable, but sound clinical practice can help to avert it in certain clinical situations" is put forward as one of the basic themes in *Prevention of Suicide*[25]. The objective of the Confidential Inquiry will begin to be met if it can assist in the clarification and development of such practice.

Appendix 2. Selected Department of Health current publications on mental health and learning disabilities

Health of the Nation

The Health of the Nation: Mental Illness Key Area Handbook (Revised edition Department of Health, 1994)

Jenkins, R. and Warman, D. *Promoting Mental Health Policies in the Workplace* (HMSO, 1993)

Mental Illness Public Information Strategy

Six booklets "*Mental Illness:...*" (1993–4)

Caring for Mentally Ill People in the Community

The Clinical Audit of Suicides and Undetermined Deaths (NHS Executive, 1994)

Working in Partnership – A Collaborative Approach to Care. Review of Mental Health Nursing (HMSO, 1994)

Patients' Perceptions Booklet: Dementia (Department of Health, 1993)

Jenkins, R. et al. *Prevention of Suicide* (HMSO. 1994)

Caring for People with a Severe Mental Illness: Information for Psychiatrists (Department of Health, 1993)

Jenkins, R. (1994) The Health of the Nation: Recent Government Policy and Legislation. *Psychiatric Bulletin*,**18**, 324–327

Good Practice in the Administration of Depot Neuroleptics – a Guidance Document for Mental Health and Practice Nurses (Department of Health /Royal College of Nursing, 1994)

Services for the Mental Health of Children and Young People in England: A National Overview (Department of Health, 1994)

Introduction of Supervision Registers for Mentally Ill People from 1 April 1994 (HSG(94)5)

Guidance on the Discharge of Mentally Disordered People and their Continuing Care in the Community (LASSL(94)4/HSG(94)27)

Draft Guide to Arrangements for Inter-agency Working for the Care and Protection of Severely Mentally Ill People (Department of Health)

A Handbook on Child and Adolescent Mental Health (DH, 1994)

Mental Health Act

Code of Practice: Mental Health Act 1983 (Revised edition HMSO, 1993)

Legal Powers on the Care of Mentally Ill People in the Community: Report of the Internal Review (DH, 1993)

Mental Health Review Tribunals for England. *Annual Report 1993* (DH 1994)

Mental Health Act Commission. *Fifth Biennial Report 1991–3* (HMSO, 1993)

Mentally Disordered Offenders

Reed Review: A Note of the Visit Programme (Vols 1–7, January 1993)

Mental Health Task Force

Various publications

Appendix 3: Examples of questionnaires

The type of questionnaire sent out to clinicians depended on whether the case involved homicide or suicide and whether the patient was in-patient, outpatient or discharged patient. Two examples are set out below: in-patient (suicide) and out-patient (homicide).

SUICIDE

IN-PATIENTS IN PSYCHIATRIC UNIT

NAME OF ENQUIRY SUBJECT: ENQUIRY NO :

PLEASE COMPLETE THIS QUESTIONNAIRE AS FULLY AS POSSIBLE. WHERE RELEVANT PLEASE TICK OR CIRCLE APPROPRIATE RESPONSE, AND WHERE FULLER ANSWERS ARE NEEDED WRITE IN THE SPACE PROVIDED ON THE SHEETS OR ON THE BACK OF THE PREVIOUS SHEET.

1.   **ABOUT THE SUBJECT**

1.1 DATE OF BIRTH: 1.2   SEX: Male/Female

1.3 MARITAL STATUS:

    1. Single   2. Married   3. Co-habiting
    4. Separated   5. Divorced   6. Widowed

1.4 EMPLOYMENT STATUS:

    1. Full-Time Education   2. Self-Employed   3. Employed
    4. Unemployed   5. Retired   6. Housewife/Husband
    7. Unemployed through chronic ill-health

1.5 ETHNIC GROUP:

    1. Caucasian   2. black-Caribbean   3. Black-African
    4. Black, other pls specify   5. Indian   6. Pakistani
    7. Bangladeshi   8. Chinese   9. Other, please describe

1.6 NHS/LOCAL AUTHORITY LOCATION:

    1. East Anglia   2. Eire   3. Mersey   4. N.E.Thames
    5. Northern   6. N.Ireland   7. N.Western   8. N.W.Thames
    9. Oxford   10. Scotland   11. S.E.Thames   12. S.Western
    13. S.W.Thames   14. Trent   15. Wales   16. Wessex
    17. W.Midlands   18. Yorkshire

1.7 PSYCHIATRIC DIAGNOSIS IN ACCORDANCE WITH ICD 10:

1.8 HAD THE PATIENT EVER HAD PREVIOUS SPECIALIST PSYCHIATRIC
     CARE PRIOR TO RECENT CONTACT?   YES\NO

     If so, any previous hospital admission?   YES\NO
     How many admissions, if known?

1.9 HAD THE PATIENT EVER RECEIVED SPECIALIST SOCIAL WORK/ SOCIAL SERVICES COMMUNITY CARE?   YES\NO

1.10 PRIOR TO PRESENT EPISODE HAD THE PATIENT EVER HAD:

Episodes of deliberate self-harm   YES\NO
Episodes of violent\aggressive behaviour, whether verbal
or physical   YES\NO

1.11 HAD THE PATIENT BEEN PRONE TO PHYSICAL ILLNESS?   YES\NO
PLEASE SPECIFY

1.12 WERE CLINICAL NOTES FROM PREVIOUS PSYCHIATRIC CARE MADE AVAILABLE?   YES\NO\N/A

1.13 INDICATE THE TYPE OF HOSPITAL WHERE PATIENT WAS BEING TREATED:

      1. Psychiatric Hospital   2. District General Hospital
      3. Interim Secure Unit   4. Regional Secure Unit
      5. Special Hospital   6. Other, please specify

1.14 WAS THERE A FAMILY HISTORY OF:
1. Suicide   YES\NO
2. Violence/Aggression   YES\NO

2.   **THE SUICIDE EVENT**

2.1 DATE, DAY AND TIME OF DEATH:

2.2 (i) METHOD, PLEASE SPECIFY

      1. Poisoning   2. Hanging   3. Jumping from height
      4. Drowning   5. Suffocation   6. Railway
      7. Self-Laceration   8. Shooting   9. Car Exhaust Gas
      10.Other
      Please indicate any features of special note

(ii) DID THE USE OF ALCOHOL OR OTHER NON-PRESCRIBED SUBSTANCES IMMEDIATELY PRECEDE THE DEATH?   YES\NO

2.3   PLACE: 1. In own hospital ward
                 2. Elsewhere in hospital
                 3. In hospital grounds
                 4. Away from hospital in normal residence
                 5. Away from hospital outside normal residence

2 . 4   IF SUICIDE OCCURRED OUTSIDE HOSPITAL GROUNDS WAS PATIENT:

           1. Absent from ward without leave
           2. Given permission to leave ward for short visit
           3. Given permission for home leave (ie. More than one day)
           4. Other, please specify

2.5   DATE OF ADMISSION TO WARD:

2.6   WHAT STAGE OF ASSESSMENT/TREATMENT HAD BEEN REACHED:
           1. Still at stage of assessment
           2. Treatment recently commenced
           3. Care & treatment well established
           4. Stage of rehabilitation reached
           5. Pre-discharge
           Other comment if necessary

2.7   CATEGORISATION OF DEATH:

       i. Coroner   1. Suicide   2. Open verdict
                            3. Accident/Misadventure   4. Other

       ii. Clinical Opinion 1. Suicide   2. Open verdict
                            3. Accident/Misadventure   4. Other

3.   **THE PATIENT IN THE PSYCHIATRIC WARD**

3.1   AT THE TIME OF THE DEATH WAS THE PATIENT:
       (i)
       1. Informal in status
       2. Informal, but subject to detention earlier in this episode of illness
       3. Compulsorily detained under the Mental Health Act, *please specify section*
       4. Detained under other legislation, please specify

(ii) IF DETAINED WAS DETENTION:
    1. Arranged before admission 2. Implemented after hospital/unit admission

3.2   HAD THE PATIENT AT ANY TIME EXPRESSED:

    1. Suicidal intentions   YES\NO
    2. Ideas of violence, aggression   YES\NO

IF NO COMPLETE QUESTION 3.3 AND CONTINUE FROM 3.9
IF YES, COMPLETE QUESTIONS 3.4 ONWARDS

3.3   1. WAS THE SUBJECT EVER RAISED WITH PATIENT?   YES\NO
        2. DID THE PATIENT DENY ANY SUICIDAL INTENTION?   YES\NO\NA
        3. DID THE PATIENT DENY ANY VIOLENT INTENTION?   YES\NO\NA

3.4 *IF YES:*
    HOW WAS THIS RAISED?
    1. Spontaneously by patient?   2. When subject was raised by another?
    PLEASE SPECIFY

3.5   HAD THE SUICIDAL IDEATION:

    1. Remained unchanged   2. Improved   3. disappeared
    4. Deteriorated   5. Fluctuated   6. Don't Know

3.6 *IF VARIABLE,*
    HAD THIS CONFUSED THE ASSESSMENT?   YES\NO\DON'T KNOW

3.7   IF THE PATIENT'S MENTAL STATE HAD IMPROVED WAS THIS:

    1. Sufficient to reassure staff about the suicide wish
    2. Despite main life problems remaining unresolved
    3. Still causing staff concern
    4. Other, please specify

3.8   WHAT OBJECTIVE EVIDENCE HAD THERE BEEN OF SERIOUSNESS
    OF SUICIDAL INTENT?
    PLEASE GIVE SPECIFIC EXAMPLES EG:

    1. Verbal expression of intent   2. Physiological symptoms of depression
    3. Behaviour

3.9 WHO HAD ASSESSED THE POTENTIAL RISK?
(Circle more than one if appropriate)

1. Consultant
2. Senior Registrar
3. Registrar or S.H.O.
4. Ward Sister/Charge Nurse
5. Staff Nurse
6. Clinical Psychologist
7. Student Nurse
8. Nurse Auxiliary
9. Occupational Therapist
10. Social Worker
11. Other, please specify
12. Not applicable

3.10 HOW OFTEN HAD THIS BEEN DONE? (INDICATE BY WHICH OF THE ABOVE)

1. Daily   2. Weekly   3. Monthly   4. Other

3.11 HOW RECENTLY HAD THIS BEEN DONE BEFORE DEATH?
(INDICATE BY BY WHICH OF THE ABOVE)

1. In last 24 hrs   2. Within 1 week   3. Within last 4 weeks   4. Other

3.12 HOW HAD IT BEEN RECORDED?   1. Verbally   2. Written

3.13 HAD THERE BEEN ANY SPECIAL PRECAUTIONS TAKEN IN RESPONSE
TO SUICIDE RISK?   YES/NO

3.14 IF YES,
WHAT WERE THEY? PLEASE SPECIFY

1. Increased supervision
2. Recommended for transfer to greater or maximum security ward
3. Transfer to greater or maximum security ward
4. Review medication
5. Use of Mental Health Act, specify section
6. Use of seclusion
7. Other

3.15 WHEN HAD THEY BEEN PUT INTO ACTION?

1. Within 24 hrs prior to death
2. Within 1 week prior to death
3. 1-4 weeks
4. 1-3 months
5. 3-6 months
6. 6-12 months

3.16 IF NO LONGER APPLICABLE, WHEN HAD THEY BEEN STOPPED?

1. Within 24 hrs prior to death 2. Within 1 week prior to death
3. 1-4 weeks 4. 1-3 months
5. 3-6 months 6. 6-12 months

3.17 HAD THERE BEEN ANY DIFFICULTIES IN TAKING THESE SPECIAL
PRECAUTIONS? YES\NO

3.18 IF YES, PLEASE SPECIFY:

1. Patient unwilling to co-operate 2. Insufficient levels of staff
3. Easy access to unsupervised areas 4. Poor Security
5. Lack of funding 6. No area of greater security available
7. ASW unwilling to make application for formal detention
8. Other, please specify

3.19 DID THE TEAM HAVE AN AGREED CODE OF PRACTICE
CONCERNING THE CARE OF SUICIDAL PATIENTS? YES\NO
IF YES, PLEASE SPECIFY:

4. **THE PSYCHIATRIC WARD**

4.1 (i) WHAT CATEGORY OF WARD WAS THE PATIENT STAYING ON
AT TIME OF DEATH?

1. Acute 2. Long stay 3. Elderly 4. Intensive care
5. Other, please specify

(ii) IF IN INTENSIVE CARE, WAS THE WARD:

1. Locked 2. Unlocked 3. Intermittently locked

4.2 NUMBER OF PATIENTS WHEN FULL?
NUMBER OF PATIENTS AT TIME OF DEATH?

4.3 WAS THE LEVEL OF NURSING STAFF UP TO COMPLEMENT? YES\NO
IF NO, PLEASE COMMENT

4.4　(i) WHAT WAS THE RATIO BETWEEN TRAINED AND UNTRAINED STAFF?

(ii) WAS THIS FELT TO BE SATISFACTORY?　　　　　　　　YES\NO
IF NO, PLEASE COMMENT

4.5　HAD THERE BEEN A CHANGE OF WARD PRIOR TO DEATH?　YES\NO
IF YES, HAD THE CHANGE OCCURRED WITHIN:

1. 24 Hours　　　　2. One week　　　　3. More than one week

4 . 6　WAS THE NUMBER OF DIFFICULT PATIENTS ABOVE AVERAGE?
IF YES, PLEASE COMMENT

EVENTS & RELATIONSHIPS

WITHIN HOSPITAL

4.7　HAD ANY EVENT SIGNIFICANT FOR THE PATIENT OCCURRED
DURING HIS/HER STAY ON THE WARD? *FOR INSTANCE*　YES\NO

1. Any event leading to loss of self esteem
2. Failure to comply with ward rules
3. Confrontation with other patients
4. Suicide In another patient
5. Deliberate self-harm in another patient
6. Another patient encouraging suicide
7. Aggressive behaviour in another patient
8. Substance abuse (including alcohol) in another patient
9. Other,
Please describe

OUTSIDE HOSPITAL

4.8　HAD ANY EVENT SIGNIFICANT FOR THE PATIENT OCCURRED
OUTSIDE HOSPITAL DURING THIS PERIOD OF PSYCHIATRIC CARE?
FOR INSTANCE　　　　　　　　　　　　　　　　　　　YES\NO

1. Break up of relationship　　　2. Death of family member
3. Eviction　　　　　　　　　　4. Redundancy
5. Child care　　　　　　　　　6. Other
Please describe

4.9 HAD THE PATIENT RECEIVED ANY VISITORS WHILE ON THE WARD?

YES\NO

IF YES, PLEASE GIVE AN INDICATION OF THE FREQUENCY OF THESE VISITS AND THE RELATIONSHIP OF THE VISITOR(S) TO THE PATIENT

4.10 *IF YES, PLEASE GIVE AN INDICATION OF THE EMOTIONAL TONE OF VISITS BY THOSE CLOSEST TO THE PATIENT:*

1. Good   2. Supportive   3. Unsatisfactory
4. Hostile   5. Marital problems

4.11 HAD THE PATIENT MADE ANY SIGNIFICANT RELATIONSHIPS WITH MEMBER(S) OF THE PSYCHIATRIC TEAM?   YES\NO

IF YES, PLEASE SPECIFY

4.12 IF YES, HAD ANY STAFF SIGNIFICANT TO THE PATIENT BEEN TRANSFERRED OR WAS ABSENT FROM THE WARD FOR OTHER REASONS, PRIOR TO THE DEATH?   YES/NO

IF YES, PLEASE SPECIFY

4.13 HAD THE PSYCHIATRIC STAFF ESTABLISHED A WORKING RELATIONSHIP WITH PATIENT'S RELATIVES\FRIENDS\CARERS?

YES/NO

SPECIFY AND REFER TO ANY DIFFICULTIES

4.14 HAD THE PATIENT MADE ANY SIGNIFICANT RELATIONSHIPS WITH ANY OTHER PATIENT?   YES/NO

PLEASE SPECIFY

4.15 IN GENERAL, DID THE PATIENT EXPERIENCE DIFFICULTY IN RELATING TO OTHERS ON THE WARD?   YES/NO

4.16 IF YES, IN WHAT WAY WAS THIS DIFFICULTY MANIFESTED BEHAVIOURALLY? IE:

1. Broke rules   2. Hostile   3. Solitary
4. Uncooperative   5. Aggressive   6. Other

PLEASE SPECIFY

4.17 HAD THE PATIENT BEEN SUBJECT TO A CARE PROGRAMME
APPROACH?   YES/NO

5   **LEAVE FROM IN-PATIENT UNIT**

AUTHORISED LEAVE

5.1   DID THE PATIENT HAVE ANY LEAVE?   YES/NO

5.2   *IF YES, WAS THE LEAVE AGREED WITH RELATIVES*   YES/NO

5.3   *IF YES, WAS THE LEAVE APPROPRIATE (IN LIGHT OF THE EVIDENCE
AVAILABLE AT THE TIME)*   YES/NO

5.4   *IF YES, WAS IT AS A RESULT OF DEMAND FROM THE PATIENT?*
                                                          YES/NO
5.5   WAS IT RELATED TO BED SHORTAGE   YES/NO

UNAUTHORISED LEAVE

5.6   DID THE PATIENT EVER GO ABSENT WITHOUT LEAVE?   YES/NO

5.7   *IF YES, HOW MANY TIMES*

5.8   WAS THE PATIENT ABSENT WITHOUT LEAVE AT TIME OF SUICIDE?
                                                          YES/NO
5.9   *IF YES, PLEASE SPECIFY*

(i)   WHAT ACTION WAS TAKEN WHEN ABSENCE NOTED?

(ii) WHAT CONTACTS WERE MADE WHEN ABSENCE NOTED?

1. Relations\friend   2. Police   3. Community Staff
4. GP   5. None   6. Other, please specify

6. **THE PATIENT'S LIFESTYLE**

PLEASE CIRCLE THE RESPONSE WHICH MOST CLOSELY DESCRIBED THE PATIENT

HOW WOULD YOU DESCRIBE THE PATIENT'S LIFESTYLE?

i.	Unsettled(job changes, residence changes)	No	Yes	Don't Know
ii.	Conflict With the Law	No	Yes	Don't Know
iii.	Abused Alcohol/Drugs/Solvents	No	Yes	Don't Know
iv.	No Adverse Features	No	Yes	Don't Know
v.	Other, please specify			

7. **THE PATIENT'S BEHAVIOUR WHILE IN HOSPITAL**

PLEASE INDICATE HOW YOU WOULD DESCRIBE YOUR PATIENT'S BEHAVIOUR DURING STAY IN HOSPITAL BY CIRCLING THE APPROPRIATE NUMBER FOR EACH DESCRIPTION:

1 = Not at All   2 = Sometimes   3 = Often   4 = Nearly Always

7(1)	Over-dependent on other people	1	2	3	4
7(2)	Lacking in confidence	1	2	3	4
7(3)	Withdrawn from others	1	2	3	4
7(4)	Not able to talk about problems/worries	1	2	3	4
7(5)	Apathetic and inactive	1	2	3	4
7(6)	Lacking In Enthusiasm for usual pastimes	1	2	3	4
7(7)	Over-sensitive to criticism	1	2	3	4
7(8)	Sullen & unfriendly	1	2	3	4
7(9)	Resentful and envious of others	1	2	3	4

7(10) Irritable or bad-tempered	1	2	3	4
7(11) Provocative or argumentative	1	2	3	4
7(12) Verbally Abusive	1	2	3	4
7(13) Physically aggressive	1	2	3	4
7(14) Unpredictable in behaviour	1	2	3	4
7(15) Unreliable at keeping promises\agreements	1	2	3	4
7(16) Variable in mood	1	2	3	4
7(17) Unable to cope with changes in routine	1	2	3	4
7(18) Getting little pleasure from life	1	2	3	4
7(19) Suspicious or untrusting	1	2	3	4
7(20) Neglecting personal hygiene	1	2	3	4
7(21) Worrying	1	2	3	4
7(22) Self pitying	1	2	3	4
7(23) Untruthful	1	2	3	4
7(24) Stubborn	1	2	3	4

8. **YOUR REACTION TO THE PATIENT**

1 = Not at All   2 = Sometimes   3 = Often   4 = Nearly Always

8(1) Did you ever think that the patient was
making more of his symptoms, than was
justified?   1   2   3   4

8(2)   Did you ever think that s/he was putting
the symptoms on?   1   2   3   4

8(3) Did you ever think that s/he was using
his/her symptoms to seek attention?   1   2   3   4

8(4) Did you ever think that s/he was
using his/her symptoms to control other
people in some way?   1   2   3   4

8(5) Did you ever think that s/he was using
his symptoms to avoid problems in some way?   1   2   3   4

| 8(6) | Did you ever worry that s/he might try to kill himself/herself? | 1 | 2 | 3 | 4 |

| 8(7) | Did you ever find yourself losing hope that things would improve? | 1 | 2 | 3 | 4 |

| 8(8) | Were there any times when you thought the patient should be discharged because he/she ought to stand on their own feet and that treatment had become counter productive? | 1 | 2 | 3 | 4 |

PLEASE INDICATE THE FEELINGS THAT YOU EXPERIENCED TOWARDS THE PATIENT DURING HIS/HER STAY IN HOSPITAL PRIOR TO HIS/HER DEATH BY CIRCLING THE APPROPRIATE NUMBER FOR EACH STATEMENT. DON'T WORRY IF YOUR ANSWERS SEEM TO CONTRADICT EACH OTHER – IT IS QUITE NORMAL TO HAVE TWO OPPOSITE FEELINGS AT THE SAME TIME.

1 = Not at All   2 = Sometimes   3 = Often   4 = Nearly Always

8(9)	"I felt worried about him/her"	1	2	3	4
8(10)	"I felt distant from him/her"	1	2	3	4
8(11)	"I felt protective towards him/her"	1	2	3	4
8(12)	"I felt caring towards him/her"	1	2	3	4
8(13)	"I felt hostile towards him/her"	1	2	3	4
8(14)	"She/he made me angry"	1	2	3	4
8(15)	"I felt resentful towards him/her"	1	2	3	4
8(16)	"I felt frustrated by him/her"	1	2	3	4
8(17)	"I felt frightened by him/her"	1	2	3	4
8(18)	"I felt sorry for him/her"	1	2	3	4
8(19)	"My feelings about him/her were variable"	1	2	3	4
8(20)	"I felt rejected by him/her"	1	2	3	4
8(21)	"She/he made me feel guilty"	1	2	3	4
8(22)	"I lost sleep over him/her"	1	2	3	4

9.　　　REVIEW OF CASE AFTER DEATH

9.1　DID ANY STAFF REVIEW FOLLOW THE DEATH?　　　YES\NO

9.2   HOW SOON AFTER THE EVENT WAS THIS HELD

      1. Within one week   2. Within one month
      3. Within six months   4. Other

9.3   WHICH PROFESSIONAL STAFF WERE INVOLVED:

      1. Consultant Psychiatrist   5. Social Worker
      2. Supporting Medical Staff   6. Occupational Therapist
      3. Nursing Staff   7. Clinical Psychologist
      4. Community Psychiatric Nurse   8. Other
      FURTHER DETAILS

9.4   WHICH OF THE ABOVE INSTITUTED THE REVIEW?

9.5   HAD THERE BEEN ANY MAJOR DIFFERENCE OF OPINION AMONG
      STAFF ABOUT THE WAY THIS PATIENT'S PROBLEMS SHOULD HAVE
      BEEN DEALT WITH?
      IF YES, PLEASE SPECIFY: YES\NO

9.6   WERE OTHER PATIENTS COUNSELLED BY PSYCHIATRIC STAFF
      FOLLOWING THE DEATH?   YES\NO

9.7   WHICH MEMBER OF THE PSYCHIATRIC TEAM HAD RESPONSIBILITY
      FOR INFORMING AND COUNSELLING THESE PATIENTS?

      1. Consultant Psychiatrist   5. Social Worker
      2. Supporting Medical Staff   6. Occupational Therapist
      3. Nursing Staff   7. Clinical Psychologist
      4. Community Psychiatric Nurse   8. None
      9. Other

9.8   WERE NEAREST RELATIVES OF THE PATIENT INFORMED BY
      PSYCHIATRIC STAFF OF THE CIRCUMSTANCES OF THE DEATH?
                                         YES\NO

9.9　IF YES, WAS IT POSSIBLE TO GIVE THIS INFORMATION IN A WAY WHICH WAS COMFORTING TO THE RELATIVES, AND WHICH HELPED THEM TO COME TO TERMS WITH THE DEATH?

YES\NO

9.10　WHICH MEMBER OF THE PSYCHIATRIC TEAM HAD RESPONSIBILITY FOR INFORMING AND COUNSELLING THESE RELATIVES?

1. Consultant Psychiatrist　　　5. Social Worker
2. Supporting Medical Staff　　6. Occupational Therapist
3. Nursing Staff　　　　　　　7. Clinical Psychologist
4. Community Psychiatric Nurse　8. Other

9.11　FOLLOWING INITIAL CONTACT, HAD THERE BEEN ANY FURTHER CONTACT FOLLOWING THE DEATH BETWEEN THESE RELATIVES AND PSYCHIATRIC UNIT?　　　　　　YES\NO
IF YES, PLEASE SPECIFY

9.12　DID THE CIRCUMSTANCES OF THE DEATH LEAD TO ANY RECOMMENDATIONS FOR CHANGES IN:

1. Physical lay-out of ward　　2. Supervision
3. Setting out Treatment Plans　4. Communications between staff
5. Admission Arrangements　　6. Use of detention under the MHA
7. Discharge Arrangements　　8. Other

PLEASE DESCRIBE

9.13　IF RECOMMENDATIONS WERE MADE, WHAT IS THEIR CURRENT STATUS?

1. Implemented
2. In the process of implementation
3. Other

PLEASE GIVE DETAILS

APART FROM ANY RECOMMENDATIONS DESCRIBED ABOVE, PLEASE TELL ME WHETHER, WITH HINDSIGHT, YOU CONSIDER THAT THERE ARE ANY OTHER WAYS IN WHICH THE LIKELIHOOD OF THIS DEATH MIGHT HAVE BEEN REDUCED

THANK YOU FOR YOUR HELP

IT HAS BEEN SUGGESTED THAT IT WOULD BE HELPFUL TO HAVE SOME DETAILS ABOUT THOSE PARTICIPATING IN THE ENQUIRY. IF YOU ARE AGREEABLE, PLEASE COMPLETE THE FOLLOWING:

1.   SEX: MALE / FEMALE   2.   AGE: 1. Under 39   2. 39–49
                                      3. 50–59   4. 60 plus

3 .   ETHNIC GROUP:

ONCE AGAIN MANY THANKS FOR YOUR HELP

HOMICIDE

WHILE UNDER PSYCHIATRIC CARE IN THE COMMUNITY

(Including out-patient care or supervision by any member of the Psychiatric
Service)

NAME OF ENQUIRY SUBJECT: ENQUIRY NO :

PLEASE COMPLETE THIS QUESTIONNAIRE AS FULLY AS POSSIBLE. WHERE
RELEVANT PLEASE TICK OR CIRCLE APPROPRIATE RESPONSE, AND
WHERE FULLER ANSWERS ARE NEEDED WRITE IN THE SPACE PROVIDED
ON THE SHEETS OR ON THE BACK OF THE PREVIOUS SHEET.

1. **ABOUT THE SUBJECT**

1.1 DATE OF BIRTH: 1.2 SEX: Male/Female

1.3 MARITAL STATUS:

1. Single   2. Married   3. Co-habiting
4. Separated   5. Divorced   6. Widowed

1.4 EMPLOYMENT STATUS:

1. Full-Time Education   2. Self-Employed   3. Employed
4. Unemployed   5. Retired   6. Housewife/Husband
7. Unemployed through chronic ill-health

1.5 ETHNIC GROUP:

1. Caucasian   2. black-Caribbean   3. Black-African
4. Black, other pls specify   5. Indian   6. Pakistani
7. Bangladeshi   8. Chinese   9. Other, please describe

1.6 NHS/LOCAL AUTHORITY LOCATION:

1. East Anglia   2. Eire   3. Mersey   4. N.E.Thames
5. Northern   6. N.Ireland   7. N.Western   8. N.W.Thames
9. Oxford   10. Scotland   11. S.E.Thames   12. S.Western
13. S.W.Thames   14. Trent   15. Wales   16. Wessex
17. W.Midlands   18. Yorkshire

1.7   PSYCHIATRIC DIAGNOSIS IN ACCORDANCE WITH ICD 10:

1.8 HAD THE PATIENT EVER HAD PREVIOUS SPECIALIST PSYCHIATRIC
CARE PRIOR TO RECENT CONTACT?:   YES\NO
If so, any previous hospital admission?   YES\NO
How many admissions, if known?

1.9 HAD THE PATIENT EVER RECEIVED SPECIALIST SOCIAL WORK/
SOCIAL SERVICES COMMUNITY CARE?   YES\NO

1.10 PRIOR TO PRESENT EPISODE HAD THE PATIENT EVER HAD:

Episodes of deliberate self-harm   YES\NO
Episodes of violent\aggressive behaviour, whether
   verbal or physical   YES\NO
Criminal convictions involving violence   YES\NO

1.11 HAD THE PATIENT BEEN PRONE TO PHYSICAL ILLNESS?   YES\NO
PLEASE SPECIFY

1.12 WAS THERE A FAMILY HISTORY OF

1. Suicide?   YES\NO
2. Violence\Aggression?   YES\NO
Please comment

1.13 WERE CLINICAL NOTES FROM PREVIOUS PSYCHIATRIC
CARE MADE AVAILABLE?   YES\NO\N/A

1.14 WAS THE PATIENT AWAITING ADMISSION TO AN
IN-PATIENT UNIT?   YES\NO
IF SO FOR HOW LONG , PLEASE SPECIFY

1.15 HAD ADMISSION TO AN IN-PATIENT UNIT BEEN SOUGHT,
BUT HAD NOT BEEN POSSIBLE BECAUSE OF LACK OF
AVAILABILITY?   YES\NO
IF SO, HOW RECENTLY?

1.16 HAD PATIENT RECEIVED IN-PATIENT CARE EARLIER
IN THIS EPISODE?   YES\NO
IF SO, HAD THE PATIENT BEEN SUBJECT TO ANY
SECTION OF THE M.H.A 1983   YES\NO
Specify section

1.17 *IF SO*, HAD THE PATIENT BEEN DETAINED EARLIER
IN THIS EPISODE?   YES\NO

1.18 *IF SO*, WERE ANY LEGAL RESTRAINTS STILL IN PLACE?   YES\NO
Please specify

1.19 HAD THE PATIENT BEEN SUBJECT TO A CARE
PROGRAMME APPROACH?   YES/NO
If so, please attach copy of care plan

107

1.20 WAS THE CARE PLAN FULLY OPERATIONAL AT TIME
OF INCIDENT? YES\NO

1.21 WHAT TYPE OF PROFESSIONAL WAS NOMINATED AS KEY WORKER?

1. Consultant   2. Senior Registrar   3. Registrar or S.H.O.
4. Ward Sister/Charge Nurse 5. Staff Nurse   6. Clinical Psychologist
7. Student Nurse   8. Nurse Auxiliary   9. Occupational Therapist
10. Social Worker   11. Other, please specify

1.22 PLEASE GIVE DATE OF LAST MEETING BETWEEN KEY WORKER AND
PATIENT

2. **THE HOMICIDE EVENT**

–IF DETAILS ARE KNOWN TO YOU–

2.1 DATE, DAY AND TIME OF HOMICIDE:
IF MORE THAN ONE VICTIM, PLEASE REPEAT QUESTIONS 2.2 & 2.3

2.2 (i) RELATIONSHIP OF VICTIM TO OFFENDER:

1. Family   2. Acquaintance
3. Member of staff, specify professional status   4. Another patient
5. Other, please specify

(ii) AGE OF VICTIM (if known)?

2.3 (i) METHOD, PLEASE SPECIFY

1. Stabbing   2. Shooting   3. Use of other weapon
4. Asphyxiation   5. Other, *please specify*

Please indicate any features of special note

(ii) DID THE USE OF ALCOHOL OR OTHER NON-PRESCRIBED
SUBSTANCES IMMEDIATELY PRECEDE THE EVENT?   YES\NO

2.4 WHAT CATEGORY OF ACCOMMODATION WAS THE PATIENT LIVING IN PRIOR TO EVENT?

1. At home with others   2. At home alone   3. In Lodgings
4. In local authority\health service home\hostel   5. Other, *pls specify*

2.5 WHAT STAGE OF ASSESSMENT/TREATMENT HAD BEEN REACHED:

1. Still at stage of assessment   2. Treatment recently commenced
3. Care & treatment well established   4. Stage of rehabilitation reached
5. Pre-discharge
Other comment if necessary

2.6 WHO ALERTED PSYCHIATRIC UNIT TO THE HOMICIDE?

1. Member of Psychiatric Team   2. Another Professional
3. Relative of the Patient   4. Another Patient
5. Police   6. Coroner
7. Other

2.7 ON WHAT DATE WAS THIS INFORMATION RECEIVED:

3.   **HOMICIDAL IDEATION WHILE UNDER PSYCHIATRIC CARE**

3.1 HAD THE PATIENT AT ANY TIME EXPRESSED:

1. Ideas of violence or aggression   YES\NO
2. Suicidal intentions   YES\NO

IF NO COMPLETE QUESTION 3.2 AND CONTINUE FROM 3.8
IF YES, COMPLETE QUESTIONS 3.3 ONWARDS

IF NO:
3.2 1. Was the subject ever raised with patient?   YES\NO
2. Did the patient deny any homicidal intention?   YES\NO\NA
3. Did the patient deny any suicidal intention?   YES\NO\NA

IF YES:

3.3 HOW WAS THIS RAISED?
   1. Spontaneously by patient?   2. When subject was raised by another?
   PLEASE SPECIFY

3.4 HAD THE AGGRESSIVE PATTERN OF BEHAVIOUR:

   1. Remained unchanged   2. Improved   3. disappeared
   4. Deteriorated   5. Fluctuated   6. Don't Know

3.5 *IF VARIABLE,*
   HAD THIS CONFUSED THE ASSESSMENT?   YES\NO\DON'T KNOW

3.6 IF THE PATIENT'S MENTAL STATE HAD IMPROVED WAS THIS:

   1. Sufficient to reassure staff about the aggression
   2. Despite main life problems remaining unresolved
   3. Still causing staff concern
   4. Other, please specify

3.7 WHAT OBJECTIVE EVIDENCE HAD THERE BEEN OF SERIOUSNESS
   OF AGGRESSIVE INTENT?   *PLEASE GIVE SPECIFIC EXAMPLES EG:*

   1. Verbal expression of intent   2. Presence of paranoid ideas or delusions
   3. Behaviour

3.8 WHO HAD ASSESSED THE POTENTIAL RISK?
   (CIRCLE MORE THAN ONE IF APPROPRIATE)

   1. Consultant   2. Senior Registrar
   3. Registrar or S.H.O.   4. Ward Sister/Charge Nurse
   5. Staff Nurse   6. Clinical Psychologist
   7. Student Nurse   8. Nurse Auxiliary
   9. Occupational Therapist   10. Social Worker
   11. Other, please specify   12. Not assessed

3.9 HOW OFTEN HAD THIS BEEN DONE? (INDICATE BY WHICH OF THE
ABOVE)

   1. Daily   2. Weekly   3. Monthly   4. Other

3.10 HOW RECENTLY HAD THIS BEEN DONE BEFORE HOMICIDE?
(INDICATE BY WHICH OF THE ABOVE)

1. In last 24 hrs 2. Within 1 week 3. Within last 4 weeks 4. Other

3.11 HOW HAD IT BEEN RECORDED? 1. Verbally 2. Written

3.12 HAD THERE BEEN ANY SPECIAL PRECAUTIONS TAKEN IN RESPONSE
TO RISK FROM PATIENTS' AGGRESSION? YES/NO

3.13 *IF YES, WHAT WERE THEY? PLEASE SPECIFY*

1. Increased supervision
2. Recommended for admission to psychiatric hospital or unit
3. Review medication
4. Use of Mental Health Act, **specify section**
5. Other

3.14 WHEN HAD THEY BEEN PUT INTO ACTION?

1. Within 24 hrs prior to homicide 2. Within 1 week 3. 1-4 weeks
4. 1-3 months 5. 3-6 months 6. 6-12 months
7. Still awaiting implementation

3.15 IF NO LONGER APPLICABLE, WHEN HAD THEY BEEN STOPPED?

1. Within 24 hrs prior to homicide 2. Within 1 week 3. 1-4 weeks
4. 1-3 months 5. 3-6 months 6. 6-12 months

3.16 HAD THERE BEEN ANY DIFFICULTIES IN TAKING THESE SPECIAL
PRECAUTIONS? YES\NO

3.17 *IF YES*, PLEASE SPECIFY:

1. Patient unwilling to co-operate 2. Insufficient levels of staff
3. Lack of funding 4. No bed vacancies
5. No appropriate crisis facilities outside hospital
6. Other, *please specify*

3.18 IF PATIENT WOULD NOT CONSENT TO ADMISSION,
(i) WAS COMPULSORY ADMISSION CONSIDERED? YES\NO
IF YES,
(ii) WAS ASW UNWILLING TO MAKE APPLICATION FOR
FORMAL DETENTION YES\NO

3.19 DID THE TEAM HAVE AN AGREED CODE OF PRACTICE
      CONCERNING THE MANAGEMENT OF AGGRESSION?   YES\NO
      IF YES, PLEASE SPECIFY:

3.20 HAD THE LEVEL OF PSYCHIATRIC STAFF BEEN ADEQUATE
      FOR SATISFACTORY SUPERVISION?   YES\NO
      IN NO, PLEASE COMMENT

4.   **EVENTS & RELATIONSHIPS**

4.1   HAD ANY EVENT SIGNIFICANT FOR THE PATIENT OCCURRED
      DURING THIS PERIOD OF PSYCHIATRIC CARE? *FOR INSTANCE?*
                                                       YES\NO

      1. Any event leading to loss of self-esteem
      2. Confrontation with other patients
      3. Another patient encouraging aggressive behaviour
      4. Aggressive behaviour in another patient
      5. Substance abuse (inc. alcohol) in another patient
      6. Other,
      PLEASE DESCRIBE

4.2   HAD ANY EVENT SIGNIFICANT FOR THE PATIENT OCCURRED
      OUTSIDE HOSPITAL DURING THIS PERIOD OF PSYCHIATRIC
      CARE?   *FOR INSTANCE*   YES\NO

      1. Break up of relationship   2. Death of family member   3. Eviction
      4. Redundancy   5. Child care   6. Other
      PLEASE DESCRIBE

4.3   HAD THE PATIENT MADE ANY SIGNIFICANT RELATIONSHIPS
      WITH MEMBER(S) OF THE PSYCHIATRIC TEAM?   YES\NO
      IF YES, PLEASE SPECIFY

4.4   HAD THE PSYCHIATRIC STAFF ESTABLISHED A WORKING
      RELATIONSHIP WITH PATIENT'S RELATIVES\FRIENDS\CARERS?
                                                       YES/NO

      SPECIFY AND REFER TO ANY DIFFICULTIES

112

4.5 HAD THE PATIENT MADE ANY SIGNIFICANT RELATIONSHIPS WITH ANY OTHER PATIENT? YES/NO
PLEASE SPECIFY

4.6 IN GENERAL, DID THE PATIENT EXPERIENCE DIFFICULTY IN RELATING TO OTHERS? YES/NO

4.7 IF YES, IN WHAT WAY WAS THIS DIFFICULTY MANIFESTED BEHAVIOURIAL? IE:

1. Broke rules   2. Hostile   3. Solitary
4. Uncooperative   5. Aggressive   6. Other
PLEASE SPECIFY

4.8 HAD THE PATIENT BEEN SUBJECT TO A CARE PROGRAMME APPROACH YES/NO

5. <u>PROBLEMS OF SUPERVISION DURING THE PERIOD OF PSYCHIATRIC CARE</u>

5.1 HAD THE PATIENT COMPLIED WITH:

(a) Arrangements for contacts with staff?   YES/NO
(b) With administration of medicines   YES/NO

5.2 HAD THERE BEEN ANY PROBLEMS DURING THIS PERIOD OF OUT-PATIENT PSYCHIATRIC CARE? YES/NO
IF YES, PLEASE SPECIFY

5.3 HAD FOLLOW UP ARRANGEMENTS BEEN MADE? YES/NO
IF NO, PLEASE GIVE REASONS FOR THIS

5.4 *IF YES, WERE THE ARRANGEMENTS CARRIED THROUGH SATISFACTORILY* YES/NO
IF NO, PLEASE SPECIFY

6.   **THE PATIENT'S LIFESTYLE**

            PLEASE CIRCLE THE RESPONSE WHICH MOST CLOSELY DESCRIBED
                              THE PATIENT

        HOW WOULD YOU DESCRIBE THE PATIENT'S LIFESTYLE?

        i.   Unsettled(job changes, residence changes)   No   Yes Don't Know

        ii.   Conflict With the Law   No   Yes Don't Know

        iii.   Abused Alcohol/Drugs/Solvents   No   Yes Don't Know

        iv.   No Adverse Features   No   Yes Don't Know

        v.   Other, please specify

7.   **THE PATIENT'S BEHAVIOUR WHILE UNDER PSYCHIATRIC CARE**

PLEASE INDICATE HOW YOU WOULD DESCRIBE YOUR PATIENT'S
BEHAVIOUR DURING PERIOD OF CARE BY CIRCLING THE APPROPRIATE
NUMBER FOR EACH DESCRIPTION:

          1 = Not at All   2 = Sometimes   3 = Often   4 = Nearly Always

7(1)   Over-dependent on other people   1   2   3   4
7(2)   Lacking In Confidence   1   2   3   4
7(3)   Withdrawn from others   1   2   3   4
7(4)   Not able to talk about problems/worries   1   2   3   4
7(5)   Apathetic and inactive   1   2   3   4
7(6)   Lacking In Enthusiasm for usual pastimes   1   2   3   4
7(7)   Over-sensitive to criticism   1   2   3   4
7(8)   Sullen & unfriendly   1   2   3   4
7(9)   Resentful and envious of others   1   2   3   4
7(10)   Irritable or bad-tempered   1   2   3   4
7(11)   Provocative or argumentative   1   2   3   4

1 = Not at All   2 = Sometimes   3 = Often   4 = Nearly Always

7(12) Verbally Abusive	1	2	3	4
7(13) Physically aggressive	1	2	3	4
7(14) Unpredictable in behaviour	1	2	3	4
7(15) Unreliable at keeping promises\agreements	1	2	3	4
7(16) Variable in mood	1	2	3	4
7(17) Unable to cope with changes in routine	1	2	3	4
7(18) Getting little pleasure from life	1	2	3	4
7(19) Suspicious or untrusting	1	2	3	4
7(20) Neglecting personal hygiene	1	2	3	4
7(21) Worrying	1	2	3	4
7(22) Self-pitying	1	2	3	4
7(23) Untruthful	1	2	3	4
7(24) Stubborn	1	2	3	4

8.   **YOUR REACTION TO THE PATIENT**

PLEASE INDICATE THE FEELINGS THAT YOU EXPERIENCED TOWARDS THE PATIENT DURING HIS/HER PERIOD OF TREATMENT PRIOR TO THE HOMICIDE BY CIRCLING THE APPROPRIATE NUMBER FOR EACH STATEMENT. DON'T WORRY IF YOUR ANSWERS SEEM TO CONTRADICT EACH OTHER – IT IS QUITE NORMAL TO HAVE TWO OPPOSITE FEELINGS AT THE SAME TIME.

1 = Not at All   2 = Sometimes   3 = Often   4 = Nearly Always

8(1) Did you ever think that the patient was making more of his symptoms, than was justified?	1	2	3	4
8(2) Did you ever think that s/he was putting the symptoms on?	1	2	3	4
8(3) Did you ever think that s/he was using his/her symptoms to seek attention?	1	2	3	4
8(4) Did you ever think that s/he was using his/her symptoms to control other people in some way?	1	2	3	4

	1 = Not at All 2 = Sometimes	**3 = Often**		**4 = Nearly Always**	

8(5)	Did you ever think that s/he was using his symptoms to avoid problems in some way?	1	2	3	4
8(6)	Did you ever worry that s/he might try to harm someone?	1	2	3	4
8(7)	Did you ever find yourself losing hope that things would improve?	1	2	3	4
8(8)	Were there any times when you thought the patient should be discharged because he/she ought to stand on their own feet and that treatment had become counter productive?	1	2	3	4
8(9)	"I felt worried about him/her"	1	2	3	4
8(10)	"I felt distant from him/her"	1	2	3	4
8(11)	"I felt protective towards him/her"	1	2	3	4
8(12)	"I felt caring towards him/her"	1	2	3	4
8(13)	"I felt hostile towards him/her"	1	2	3	4
8(14)	"She/he made me angry"	1	2	3	4
8(15)	"I felt resentful towards him/her"	1	2	3	4
8(16)	"I felt frustrated by him/her"	1	2	3	4
8(17)	"I felt frightened by him/her"	1	2	3	4
8(18)	"I felt sorry for him/her"	1	2	3	4
8(19)	"My feelings about him/her were variable"	1	2	3	4
8(20)	"I felt rejected by him/her"	1	2	3	4
8(21)	"She/he made me feel guilty"	1	2	3	4
8(22)	"I lost sleep over him/her"	1	2	3	4

9.   REVIEW OF CASE AFTER HOMICIDE

9.1   DID ANY STAFF REVIEW FOLLOW THE HOMICIDE?   YES\NO

9.2   HOW SOON AFTER THE EVENT WAS THIS HELD

    1. Within one week   2. Within one month
    3. Within six months   4. Other

9.3   WHICH PROFESSIONAL STAFF WERE INVOLVED:

1. Consultant Psychiatrist   5. Social Worker
2. Supporting Medical Staff   6. Occupational Therapist
3. Nursing Staff   7. Clinical Psychologist
4. Community Psychiatric Nurse   8. other
FURTHER DETAILS

9.4   WHICH OF THE ABOVE INSTITUTED THE REVIEW?

9.5   HAD THERE BEEN ANY MAJOR DIFFERENCE OF OPINION AMONG
      STAFF ABOUT THE WAY THIS PATIENT'S PROBLEMS SHOULD HAVE
      BEEN DEALT WITH?   YES\NO
      IF YES, PLEASE SPECIFY:

9.6   HAD THERE BEEN ANY FURTHER CONTACT BETWEEN THE
      PSYCHIATRIC UNIT AND RELATIVES OF THE PATIENT?   YES\NO

9.7   DID THE CIRCUMSTANCES OF THE HOMICIDE LEAD TO ANY
      RECOMMENDATIONS FOR CHANGES IN:

1. Supervision   2. Setting out Treatment Plans
3. Communications between staff   4. Admission Arrangements
5. Use of detention under the MHA   6. Discharge Arrangements
7. Other
PLEASE DESCRIBE

9.8   IF RECOMMENDATIONS WERE MADE, WHAT IS THEIR CURRENT
STATUS?

1. Implemented
2. In the process of implementation
3. Other

PLEASE GIVE DETAILS

APART FROM ANY RECOMMENDATIONS DESCRIBED ABOVE, PLEASE TELL ME WHETHER, WITH HINDSIGHT, YOU CONSIDER THAT THERE ARE ANY OTHER WAYS IN WHICH THE LIKELIHOOD OF THIS DEATH MIGHT HAVE BEEN REDUCED

IT HAS BEEN SUGGESTED THAT IT WOULD BE HELPFUL TO HAVE SOME DETAILS ABOUT THOSE PARTICIPATING IN THE ENQUIRY. IF YOU ARE AGREEABLE, PLEASE COMPLETE THE FOLLOWING:

1. SEX: MALE / FEMALE

2. AGE:

    1. Under 39   2. 39–49
    3. 50–59   4. 60 Plus.

3. ETHNIC GROUP:

ONCE AGAIN MANY THANKS FOR YOUR HELP

Appendix 4. Advertisement placed in *Compassionate Friends Newsletter*

An Inquiry set up jointly by the Government and the Royal College of Psychiatrists is reviewing deaths by suicide among people receiving specialist psychiatric care.

Dr William Boyd, Director of the Inquiry, is hoping to obtain information from the relatives of people who have died by suicide while being treated by the specialist psychiatric service in hospital or in the community. If anyone would like to help with this study and to answer a short questionnaire on a totally confidential basis, they are invited to make contact with Dr Boyd at: P.O. Box 1515, London SW1X 8P or by phone on 071-823 1031.

Appendix 5. Letter sent to colleagues in Northern Ireland

Dear Colleague,

I am most grateful to Professor McClelland for helping me to make contact with you in connection with the Confidential Enquiry which has been set up to examine the circumstances of suicides among people being treated within the psychiatric services and also those discharged from such care within the previous twelve months. The Enquiry has been set up by the Department of Health in England but is designed to cover the United Kingdom and is strongly supported by the College.

We are asking consultant psychiatrists and other professional staff involved in such cases to let us have information, on a completely confidential basis, from which we may make generalised recommendations about clinical management.

The questionnaire which is attached deals with a range of topics affecting the patient's life prior to the suicide, and is based on one already used successfully in the survey carried out by Professor Gethin Morgan in Bristol. I appreciate that it will take time to complete but, assuming that suicide in a patient is fortunately uncommon in the clinical practice of any one practitioner, I believe that it is reasonable to ask for your help in obtaining information which should provide material which can be of value to ourselves and to our patients in the future.

The final item on the questionnaire summarizes the purpose of the Enquiry, asking whether with all the benefits of hindsight you consider that there are any ways in which the likelihood of this death might have been reduced.

Your help will be much appreciated.

Yours sincerely,

W.D.Boyd

References

1. Department of Health (1992) HMSO. ISBN 0-10-119862-0.
2. North East Thames & South East Thames Regional Health Authorities (1994) *The Report of the Inquiry into the Care and Treatment of Christopher Clunis.* ISBN 0-11-7071798-1.
3. The Zito Trust (1995) *Learning the Lessons.* Mental Health Inquiry Reports published in England and Wales between 1969–1994 and their recommendations for improving practice.
4. National Health Service and Community Care Act 1990.
5. Confidential Inquiry into Homicide and Suicide by Mentally Ill People (1994) *A Preliminary Report on Homicide.* ISBN 0-902241 75 3.
6. Morgan, H. G. & Priest, P. (1991) Suicide and other unexpected deaths among psychiatric in-patients. *British Journal of Psychiatry*, **158**, 368–374.
7. HC [90] 23/LASSL [90] 11.
8. Foster, T. & McClelland, R. J. (Unpublished) A Study of Suicide in Northern Ireland by Psychological Autopsy.
9. Charlton, B., Kelly, S., Dunnell, K., *et al* (1993) Suicide deaths in England and Wales: Trends in factors associated with suicide deaths. *Population Trends*, **71**, 34–42.
10. Kingdon, D. (1992) Advances in Psychiatric Practice – Making Care Plans Work. *Population Trends*, **69**.
11. Creed, F. (1995) How consultants manage their time. *Advances in Psychiatric Treatment*, **1**, 65–70.
12. Eastman, N. (1995) Anti-therapeutic Community Mental Health Law. *British Medical Journal*, **310**, 1081–1082.
13. Monahan, J. & Steadman, H. J. (eds) (1994) *Violence and Mental Disorder. Developments in Risk Assessment.* Chicago: University of Chicago Press.
14. Bowden, P. (1990) Homicide. In *Principles and Practice of Forensic Psychiatry* (eds R. Blueglass & P. Bowden), Edinburgh: Churchill Livingstone.
15. Hafner, H. & Boker, W. (1973) Crimes of Violence by Mentally Abnormal Offenders. A psychiatric and epidemiological study in the Federal German Republic (trans Marshall, H., 1982)
16. West, D. J. (1965) *Murder followed by Suicide.* London: Heinemann.
17. Brittain, R. P. (1970) The Sadistic Murderer. *Medicine, Science and the Law*, **10**, 198–207.
18. Appleby, L. (1992) Suicide in psychiatric patients: risk and prevention. *British Journal of Psychiatry*, **161**, 749–758.
19. Barraclough, B.M., Bunch, J., Nelson, B. & Sainsbury, P. (1974) A hundred cases of suicide: clinical aspects. *British Journal of Psychiatry*, **125**, 355–373.
20. Morgan, H. G. & Priest, P. (1991) Suicide and other unexpected deaths among psychiatric in-patients. *British Journal of Psychiatry*, **158**, 368–374.
21. Crammer, J. l. (1984) The special characteristics of suicide in hospital in-patients. *British Journal of Psychiatry*, **145**, 460–463.
22. Goldacre *et al* (1993) *Lancet*, 342, 283–286.
23. Strahan, S. A. K. (1983) *Suicide & Insanity.* London: Swan & Sonnenschein & Company.
24. Barraclough, B. M., Bunch, J., Nelson, B. & Sainsbury, P. (1974) A hundred cases of suicide: clinical aspects. *British Journal of Psychiatry*, **125**, 355–373.
25. Jenkins, R., *et al* (1994) *The Prevention of Suicide.* HMSO ISBN 0 11 321690 4.